CHINESE
PHILOSOPHY

·K·U·P·E·R·A·R·D·

Published in Great Britain by
Kuperard, an imprint of Bravo Ltd
59 Hutton Grove, London N12 8DS
www.kuperard.co.uk
Enquiries: office@kuperard.co.uk

Series Editor Geoffrey Chesler
Design Bobby Birchall

ISBN 978 1 85733 489 0

British Library Cataloguing in Publication Data
A CIP catalogue entry for this book
is available from the British Library.

Printed in Malaysia

Cover image: Detail from a coloured engraving of Zhou Wenju's
original painting *A Literary Garden*. Southern Tang, tenth
century. Private Collection/The Bridgeman Art Library

Image on page 99 © Georges Jansoone, reproduced under
Creative Commons Attribution licence 3.0

CHINESE PHILOSOPHY

觸袖野石多目森
避人出島不成峰

Peter H. Nancarrow

⊘ Contents

Map: Territories of the Warring States — 7
Introduction — 8

Chapter 1: The Earliest Traces — 10
- Geography — 11
- The Archaeological Evidence — 12
- The Ancestors — 13
- The Emergence of the Bronze Age in China — 15
- The Oracle Bones — 17

Chapter 2: The *Yijing* — 20
- The Occultists — 20
- The Tradition of Divination — 21
- The Earliest Manual of Divination — 22

Chapter 3: Daoism — 24
- Laozi and the *Dao-de Jing* — 24

Chapter 4: The Teaching of Zhuangzi — 30
- Zhuangzi: The Man and the Book — 30

Chapter 5: Confucius — 36
- The Need for Administration — 36
- Confucius the Man — 38
- The *Analects* of Confucius — 40
- Confucianism in Government — 46

Chapter 6: Mozi, the First Opponent of Confucius — 50
- The Point at Issue — 50
- Mo Di's Background — 50
- Mo Di's Arguments — 53

Chapter 7: Mencius, Exponent of Confucius' Ideas — 56
- Mencius the Man — 56
- The Book of Mencius — 57
- The Goodness of Human Nature — 58
- The Mandate of Heaven — 60
- Mencius's Rebuttal of Mozi — 68

Chapter 8: Xünzi, Critic of Mencius — 71
- Xünzi the Man — 71
- The Book of Xünzi — 71
- A Pragmatic Approach to the Rites and Music — 76
- The Importance of Correct Definitions — 77
- Xünzi's Influence on Philosophy — 78

Chapter 9: The School of Names 80
- The Need to Define Things 80
- Gong-sun Long and the White Horse Debate 81
- Significance of the School of Names 86

Chapter 10: Legalism 88
- The Warring States 88
- Shang Yang 90
- Han Fei 93
- Li Si 98
- The State of Qin 99

Chapter 11: The Rise and Fall of the Empire of Qin 102
- A Unified China 102
- Evidence of the Legalism of the Qin Empire 104
- The Death of Qin Shi Huang Di and the Collapse of the Qin Empire 108
- The Rise of Han 110

Chapter 12: Buddhism in China 114
- The Arrival of Buddhism 114
- The Rise of Buddhism from Han to Sui 117
- Buddhism under the Tang 118
- The Consolidation of Confucianism 124

Chapter 13: The Neo-Confucian Synthesis 126
- Tang Confucianism 126
- Transition to Neo-Confucianism 129

Chapter 14: From Tang to Qing 132
- The Historical Perspective 132
- The Opium Wars and the Tai Ping Rebellion 136

Chapter 15: The End of the Confucian Empire 144
- Attempts at Reform 144
- The Final Collapse of the Qing Dynasty 149

Chapter 16: Philosophy after the Empire 154
- Western Philosophy in China 154
- The Birth of Communism in China 156

Chapter 17: Philosophy after Mao 158
- The Rise of a Market Economy 158
- The Re-emergence of Tradition 160
- Where Now? 162

Notes   164
Appendix: Timeline of Major Philosophers   164
Further Reading   165
Index   166

List of Illustrations

On a Mountain Path in Spring (detail). Painting by Ma Yuan,
Sung Dynasty   3
Painted jar, late Neolithic period (3300–2200 BCE)   12
The Yellow Emperor. Mural from the Han Dynasty, *c.* 151 CE   14
Shang period (1600–1027 BCE) bronze ritual vessel   16
Shang period oracle bone inscription   17
Shang period bronze head from Sanxingdui   18
Zhou period oracle bone inscription   22
Laozi leaves for the Western Hills   24
Zhuangzi   30
Zhuangzi and the butterfly   35
Confucius   38
Mo Di (Mozi)   51
Mengzi (Mencius)   56
Xünzi   71
Gon-sun Long   81
Laced bamboo 'book'   83
Shangyang   90
Han Fei   94
Painted reconstruction of Qin terracotta archer   99
Head of terracotta Qin soldier   101
Qin Shi Huang Di, first emperor of a united China   103
Terracotta soldiers in Qin Shi Huang Di's mausoleum   109
Bronze figure of a flying horse, Han dynasty   113
Statue of the Buddha, Liao dynasty, tenth century CE   116
Painting of Tai Zong, Sung dynasty, *c.* 1000 CE   119
Han Yu   124
Zhu Xi   130
The Jesuit observatory, Beijing   133
Lord Macartney's audience with Qian Long   135
Hong Xiuchuan, founder of the Tai Ping movement   139
The Dowager Empress Yehonala   145
Boxer rebel   148
Sun Yat Sen   151
Mao Zedong   157

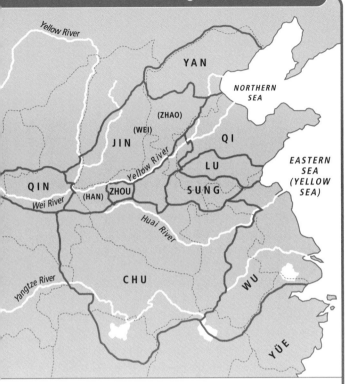

In recent years, China has emerged as a superpower and Westerners have suddenly had to come to terms with a powerful nation whose ancient civilization owes little to outside influences. For the West, China has been remote in many ways. We have felt its culture to be alien, its people inscrutable. Its language, and particularly its writing system, are totally different from our own. To understand modern China we need to overcome our sense of 'otherness' and appreciate what lies behind the way in which Chinese people think.

Historically, Europeans have long benefited from Chinese inventions and discoveries – paper, silk, porcelain, the compass and gunpowder, to name but a few. It is often held that these practical developments sprang from Daoism, one of the main strands of early Chinese philosophy. The Daoists believed that Man should follow the 'grain' of nature rather than cut across it, and in the course of discovering what this 'grain' was they investigated natural forces and materials, and experimented widely to find out how these could be utilised. Their respect for nature resonates strongly with the ecological ideas of today.

Another strand of Chinese philosophy, Confucianism, was more concerned with the relationships between people, and saw its task as working out how a populous society could live in harmony. Confucius and his followers argued for a system of mutual respect, where each individual owed duties to some and responsibilities to others, in a social order where, indeed, no man was an island. Individualism would be subordinated to the good of the community, and all people would be provided for.

The third main strand of Chinese philosophy was Buddhism: a late arrival on the scene in historical terms, but one that focused on Man's relationship to the cosmos. It succeeded in China because of its resonance with philosophical Daoism, but the Buddhist concept of compassion for all creation added the extra dimension of Man's relationship to Man to the Daoist quest to understand the Unchanging Way and the virtue of *wu-wei*, which means 'achieving without exertion'.

The complex interaction of these philosophical traditions came to influence all aspects of life in China. They continue – even under Communism – to underpin much of Chinese thinking and behaviour. The study of Chinese philosophy will bring even greater rewards than the expediency of doing so. The wealth of Chinese thought and literature is not of historical or intellectual interest only. It contains profound insights into the human condition and offers challenging perspectives on our place as humans in society, in nature and in the cosmos.

Chapter 1

The Earliest Traces

In approaching the story of Chinese philosophy, it is important to be aware that an identifiably Chinese culture has had a documented existence that spans some 4,000 years. Indeed, there are even older archaeological traces which suggest that its roots may extend at least 2,000 or 3,000 years further back than that, so Chinese cultural patterns pre-date the existence of a single political entity that can be called China, since the unified state only came into being in 221 BCE. For convenience, however, we shall use the term 'China' as a convenient shorthand to describe the geographical area now known as China, and 'Chinese' to identify its inhabitants.

As in many cultures, there were those in China who tried to work out the ways in which individuals should conduct themselves and rulers should govern the people. From the earliest times, scholars and teachers who developed philosophical thought were aware of traditional occult systems, so philosophy and religious thought became intertwined in a cultural environment which they thought extended back to a legendary era. As the development of philosophical thought in China was mainly concerned with matters of government and social organisation, the three strands of philosophy, religion and politics were woven together, sometimes close-knit and sometimes more loosely associated. Moreover, within each strand there were competing views.

This ongoing blend of influences, and the relative importance of each strand at any time, can be traced throughout Chinese history right up to the present day, and so in following the story of Chinese philosophy we shall be touching on archaeology, history, geography, philosophy, religion, statecraft and politics, to discover how the philosophy developed and how China in the twenty-first century is still influenced by this remarkable continuity of culture and thought.

Geography

The geography of China ensured that the development of society took place in substantial isolation from the rest of the world. To the east and south-east lay the China Sea and the Pacific, to the north lay the steppes and tundra, to the west and north-west there were the central Asian deserts, to the west loomed Tibet and the Himalayan range, and to the south-west the jungles provided another natural barrier to free travel and migration.

The Archaeological Evidence

Against this backdrop, the first Neolithic settlements grew up in the Yellow River valley in north China. As evidence to support the assertion that the development of Chinese culture rose in isolation, archaeological excavations have yielded stone tools of a different pattern from that of Western tools. The tools found in China have a distinctive cutting edge formed by chipping from both faces of the tool, compared with the chipping from one face typical of the West.

Neolithic culture (*c.* 7000–2000 BCE) became quite widespread, extending from sites in modern-day Gansu province, where painted red pottery was found, to Longshan near the mouth of the Yellow River and sites as far south as Hangzhou below the Yangtze River, where a distinctive black pottery has been excavated. Despite the differences in the manufacturing process that resulted in the different colours of the body of the ceramics, however, the detailed stylistic features of the wares indicate that they come from a generally uniform cultural background.

The early ceramic finds cannot in themselves tell us anything about the modes of philosophical thought that their makers possessed, but there are examples of Neolithic pottery with graphs incised into them which correspond closely to modern Chinese characters, indicating that a written form of language clearly linked to Chinese was probably in use during the Neolithic period. Another find of incised tortoise shells carrying recognizable characters indicates, on the basis of radiocarbon dating, that divination was almost certainly being practised as long ago as 5000 BCE.

So we can say with some degree of certainty that a distinctive proto-Chinese society was developing around and to the south of the Yellow River during the Neolithic period, that the people spoke a language from which Chinese would evolve, and that it probably had a shamanistic culture related among other things to divination using tortoise shells.

The Ancestors

The importance of the clan is a distinct feature of Chinese communities, and the significance of 'the ancestors' is clear from a number of discoveries dating from the dawn of Chinese written material in the Shang period (1766–1027 BCE), whether oracle bone inscriptions or inscriptions on bronze objects. This combination of divination and ancestor worship not only contributed to the continuation of occult practices, but also provided a formal framework in which they would persist in China long after the downfall of the Shang state. Detailed sources for occultism only survive from later periods, but the archaeological evidence is clearly consistent with a pre-Shang origin of the practices that were documented later.

The ties of clan also determined other hierarchical structures in society, including the relationship between the ruler of a state and his subjects. These

relationships were at the heart of the early legends
that defined the intellectual picture the Chinese had
of their origin as a people.

Concepts of state rule and administration were
reflected in the legends, starting from Pan
Gu, the supposed creator of the world.
According to the legends, Pan Gu
was followed by a series of rulers,
the Emperor of Heaven, the
Emperor of Earth and the Emperor
of Humanity, and then by two key
figures, Fu Xi, the patron of hunting and
animal husbandry, and Shen Nong, the
patron of agriculture. The last of the
purely legendary figures was the
Yellow Emperor, Huang Di. The names
give clear clues to the legendary
nature of these figures; for example, the name Shen
Nong means 'spirit farmer'.

It is the next three generations of legendary figures,
the 'model kings', who are of interest to us, because
they are more easily identifiable with human rather
than supernatural beings – and while we cannot
identify any historical individual on the basis of the
legendary accounts, it is by no means impossible that
the behaviour of individual chieftains was perpetuated
in legend. The names of the model kings are Yao, Shun
and Yu. Yao was considered to have been a benevolent
ruler, but his reputation rests on the story that he
passed his responsibilities to Shun, a meritorious
fisherman, rather than to his son, who would normally
have inherited his father's position. In turn, Shun

abdicated and handed the throne to Yu, a commoner. According to the legends the choice of Yu was auspicious despite his lowly origins, as he had managed to subdue a mighty flood that had inundated China by creating a network of drainage and irrigation systems throughout the country. The story was that he spent nine years away from his home carrying out this task, wading in water for so long that he had no hair left on his calves.

The tales of Yao, Shun and Yu 'the Great' (as he became known) were highly influential in Chinese thought in setting the pattern of ideal kingship, and their significance was expounded by perhaps the most famous of all Chinese philosophers, Confucius.

The Emergence of the Bronze Age in China

As the Neolithic period continued, settlements grew larger, and there is evidence that they supported specialised craftsmen's quarters as well as housing the workers who were engaged in the agricultural activities needed to supply food for their inhabitants. The settlements were walled, and the massive size of these walls, some being up to nearly 33 feet (10 metres) high and correspondingly thick, clearly involved much labour and the managerial expertise needed to organise it. This development in society paved the way for the two major strands of indigenous Chinese philosophical thought, namely the nature-based/agrarian Daoism on the one hand and the hierarchical/administrative Confucianism on the other. Both these strands were to continue into the Bronze

Age, when the Shang state came to supremacy among the other local rulers.

The Shang period is often referred to as the Shang Dynasty, but this terminology is perhaps misleading. The supremacy of the Shang regime over neighbouring powers was not achieved by conquest, but by the tactic of the punitive raid, a strategy by which neighbouring communities could be kept in check against attacking the Shang.

The technology that enabled the Shang rulers to maintain their position for a period of about 750 years was the working of bronze. It is believed that the technology filtered through the central Asian deserts towards China, since very small, very early bronze castings have been found in north-west China. In the hands of the Shang bronzesmiths, however, the technology of bronze working developed in little more than sixty years to reach such a level of technical expertise and artistic excellence that from early in the Shang period very large castings were being made, and with a decoration and finish that has never been rivalled since in China. Quite apart from the financial power this technology offered, and the high reputation of the state that controlled it, many of the earliest bronze artefacts discovered by archaeologists are weapons, including swords, spears, arrow-heads and the typically Chinese halberd or 'dagger-axe', the *ge* – clearly, the Shang fighters were going to be a formidable enemy in time of conflict.

Their fighting units would be highly mobile as well, having chariots that we know of from chariot burials, including bronze working parts.

The Oracle Bones

Archaeological findings also provide evidence of the existence of the two modes of thought that continued throughout the Shang period. This evidence takes the form of so-called 'oracle bones', which are variously sheep and ox shoulder blades, and tortoise shells. Their mode of use seems bizarre to the modern reader, but demonstrates a consistent pattern that makes clear that divination by 'scapulimancy' (the reading of shoulder blades) was an accepted part of Shang life. What happened was this. If somebody wanted to discover the answer to a question (when would it be auspicious to go hunting, when should a particular sacrifice be made, and so on), they would go to the diviner and pose the question to him. The diviner would then take a shoulder blade (for everyday use – tortoise shell was for grander occasions) and place a heated metal point on a shallow cavity worked into the bone. The heat from the point was sufficient to cause the bone or shell to crack from the thermal shock, and the diviner would then 'interpret' the pattern of cracks to give the answer to the question. The jackpot hit by the archaeologists was to find examples in which the question and/or the answer had been incised on the bone or shell. From a mass of oracle bone inscriptions it has been possible to discover a great deal about sociological, personal and administrative life under the Shang. One set of oracle bones even included the names of the kings of Shang, and remarkably the list was found to be substantially identical to the list proposed in the *Shiji* by its compiler, the historian Si-ma Qian, in 90 BCE – a posthumous triumph, since the authenticity of his list had been doubted, and ridiculed by some, until he was vindicated by the Anyang excavations.

Si-ma Qian held the office of Grand Historian in the Western Han Dynasty. His *Shiji* (literally, 'historical record') is still published today and constitutes one of the major sources for early Chinese history. It was conceived as a complete history of China down to his own time, but also includes a number of technical treatises relevant to state administration. We shall have reason to refer to it later on a number of occasions.

Another well-known archaeological site contemporary with the later Shang period, at Sanxingdui in Sichuan province, has yielded ivory, jade and bronze artefacts with strong clues to a shamanistic tradition. Among the finds was a huge bronze standing figure, which has been interpreted by some scholars as an image of a shaman, together with many cast bronze heads in a similar style. There are parallels with later miniature bronzes from the early part of the Zhou Dynasty, the regime that conquered the Shang in the eleventh century BCE and administered the state by delegating authority in each area to family members of the Zhou clan. This continuity of such bronzes into the early, or 'Western', Zhou period again stresses the long continuity in China of such ideas.

Continuity of the two traditions, the nature-based/agrarian and the hierarchical/administrative, can therefore be proved, although despite the development of written records on bone and shell, no written treatises on philosophy from the Shang period have survived.

In the next historical period, however, the formalisation of statehood in the Western Zhou meant that the hierarchical aspect of Chinese thought would become increasingly important. This is confirmed by the increasing number of written records from the Western Zhou whose contents have survived to the present day.

Chapter 2

The *Yijing*

The Occultists

In contrast to those who sought a hierarchical organisation of society, the occultists paved the way for the nature-based school of Daoism. Although the fundamental texts date from around 300 BCE, they appear to include some much older material. For example, a book known as the *Liezi* may contain material from the fifth century BCE, while another, known as the *Guanzi*, refers to a man who died in 645 BCE. The *Liezi* mentions Yang Zhu, who was reputed to have been a recluse, and in a work of the third century BCE he is referred to as 'a man whose policy it is not to enter a city which is in danger, nor to remain in the army. Even for the great profit of the whole world, he would not exchange one hair of his shank. He is one who despises things and values life.'

This withdrawal from the life of society was the consequence of a total focus on nature, and a wish to align oneself with the order of the natural world. It was a way of thinking that viewed most human activity as being in conflict with nature, and indeed saw Man's 'action' as directly contrary to the 'inaction' that characterised the natural order. The natural order of the world became known among followers of these ideas as 'the Way' or, in Chinese, *Dao*.

The Tradition of Divination

The transition from the Shang period to its successor, the Western Zhou, marked the beginning of a relatively stable period of some 250 years, during which many of the underlying cultural features of China continued unaltered. As in the case of the Shang, the Zhou rulers did not attempt to control the whole area directly from a central capital but parcelled out the territory to be ruled by vassal kings chosen from the ruling clan of Zhou, who owed allegiance to the central authority. There was considerable cultural continuity; ceramic manufacture and bronze casting continued, although the latter rarely achieved the level of technical expertise of the Shang, and archaeological evidence of animism and shamanism in the Western Zhou period has come to light – for example, in the miniature bronze figures from Baoji Rujiazhuang in Shaanxi province.

This strand of Chinese intellectual culture, which, as we have seen, originated in the agricultural tradition of the Neolithic, is older than the city-state culture of the Shang, from which the more socially and politically flavoured strands like Confucianism arose. However, it would inevitably have been a broader approach to life than an administrative theory relevant to a small ruling class, so although written sources for Chinese occultism only appear much later in history, it is appropriate to discuss it here.

One work whose philosophy almost certainly stretches back to the earliest shamanism and divinatory practices is the *Zhouyi*, a short book which includes instruction for the interpretation of patterns of three or six full and broken lines, the trigrams and hexagrams. It is held by some scholars that the trigrams and hexagrams derive directly from the oracle bone divinatory practices, and that the drawing of long (full-line) and short (broken-line) sticks is related to the types of cracks seen in the oracle bones.

The Earliest Manual of Divination

The date of the *Zhouyi* itself is not easy to determine accurately, but it may come from as long ago as 700 BCE. Originally the patterns of three lines were used as the basis of divination, each line being either full (*yang*) or broken (*yin*), but at an early date the groups of three lines were combined to create groups of six lines, which would enable sixty-four different combinations to be set up. As a method of divination, the diviner or his subject would select six milfoil stalks at random from a batch consisting of both long (*yang*) and short (*yin*) stalks; the diviner would then cast them into a hexagram and give the divination. The *Zhouyi* contained a list of all the possible hexagrams, with a gnomic commentary on each, so that the individual could attempt his own divination without the need to engage a shaman. The *Yijing* (or *I Ching*), which incorporates the *Zhouyi*, is still available in bookshops today.

The *Zhouyi* represents only one of a number of occult practices that are known to have existed in China. Again, we do not have early documentary evidence of these practices, but archaeological evidence confirms the early origin of what was written later. A source from the Han Dynasty lists six classes of occult arts: 1) astrology; 2) almanacs and portents; 3) Five Element theory; 4) divination by bones and milfoil stalks; 5) other divination practices; and 6) forms, which included physiognomy and *fengshui*. These six 'schools' formed the basis for the Yin-yang theory.

Although referred to as 'occultism', these schools of thought are important in the intellectual history of China, since the Five Element theory and the Yin-yang school, which was later to evolve from the six occult arts, would both become instrumental in early empirical attempts to understand the physical world. Indeed, this part of the occult tradition may have been fed by the early technologies that arose in China in relation to ceramics and bronze smelting, and in turn may have added impetus to the transition to iron casting.

To summarise, it is clear from archaeological and other evidence that occult practices continued to be practised during the Western Zhou period, and that nature-based schools of thought were alive and well in China at this time.

Chapter 3

Daoism

Laozi and the *Dao-de Jing*

The written origins of Daoism are to be found in a book which was originally entitled *Laozi* but later called the *Dao-de Jing*. The title *Laozi* was long understood to be the name of its compiler, but from the historical sources it is impossible to identify any individual who corresponds to the Laozi of the book. Even the usually well-informed Si-ma Qian, who wrote the definitive history of China, the *Shiji*, published in 90 BCE, admitted in his biography of Laozi that it was impossible to know what was the truth.

It is perhaps significant that the literal translation of Laozi is 'old master', and there is some evidence that a number of books written at around the same time as the *Laozi* had similar titles, imputing the wisdom of age to their content. On this basis we can say that there probably never was a person called Laozi who wrote the work of that name, but in the China of 300 BCE the mere existence of a book with that title would have carried the presumption that it had indeed been written by such an individual. The total absence of any trace of 'Laozi' himself puts him into the realm of the legendary sages, but in Daoist tradition his alleged date of birth positions him as a predecessor of Confucius – an assertion which was probably not accidental, despite the fact that most of the extant works of Daoism are later than the time of Confucius.

Despite the uncertainty around the actual person of Laozi, the content of the book that carries the name is clearly consistent with the nature-based philosophy and occultism that had come down through the Western Zhou (*c.* 1100–770 BCE) and Spring and Autumn (*c.* 722-481 BCE) periods. It does, however, mark a shift from the earlier occult schools towards a mysticism that would characterise the formal Daoist school.

This formal Daoism takes its name from the character *dao*, meaning a way or path. It was the belief of the Daoists that there is a path or 'grain' of nature that the followers of Daoism should strive to follow. The Dao itself was seen as mysterious and unknowable; indeed, the very first couplet of the *Dao-de Jing* is:

道可道非常道
Dao ke dao fei chang Dao

名可名非常名
Ming ke ming fei chang ming

The character *ming* at the beginning of the second line of the couplet means 'a name', and the couplet can be translated into English as:

> *A Way which can be defined as 'Way' is not the changeless Way.*
> *A name which can be defined as the name [of the Way] is not the name of the changeless.*

So the starting point of the *Dao-de Jing*, which is the master document for all subsequent Daoist thinking, is that the fundamental way of nature is unknowable and un-nameable.

Another concept basic to Daoist philosophy is the concept of non-action, or *wu-wei*. The classic statement is in Section 37 of the *Dao-de Jing*, which begins:

> *The Dao is always without action,*
> *yet there is nothing which is not done.*

This is telling us that the world's 'grain' of Dao is self-sufficient for the world to function, and that there is no need for specific activity on the part of Dao.

The book then goes on in its next section to point out that non-action should also be characteristic of human beings:

> *One of superior virtue practices inaction,*
>   *and there is nothing left to do;*
> *One of inferior virtue acts on something,*
>   *and things remain to be done.*

Some light may be shed on the concept of *wu-wei* by another section of the *Dao-de Jing*, where the point at issue appears to be the problems which can arise from over-exertion:

> *One who stands on tiptoe has no stability,*
> *One who strides out does not progress steadily,*
> *One who is self-centred will not make a good*
>   *impression,*
> *One who is self-righteous will not be respected,*
> *One who is self-aggrandising achieves no success,*
> *One who exaggerates his qualities will not endure.*
> *From the standpoint of Dao one can say*
>   *'Excess food and accumulated baggage are to*
>   *be abhorred',*
> *So the followers of Dao do not associate with*
>   *such things.*

The actions that are criticised in this passage exemplify self-defeating attempts to achieve some result. The first two are simple to understand, but they set the scene for the following examples, which are concerned with excesses of personal behaviour that are aimed to impress the onlooker but, because they set up an overblown reputation, will in the end fail as the true nature of the person becomes clear. All these attitudes are seen as failure to follow the Dao of how things are. Coupled with the previously quoted section, we can see how *wu-wei*, non-action, becomes a concept that involves not pushing against what is – the undesirable action is that which would attempt to work against or across the natural Dao of things.

A different take on the quality of 'absence' implicit in *wu-wei* is to be found in Section 11 of the *Dao-de Jing*:

Thirty spokes may converge on the wheel's hub,
But it is the space in the centre which connects
   to the cart.
A lump of clay becomes a vessel,
But it is the space in the centre which makes
   it a vessel.
Construct doors and windows for a room,
But it is the apertures which make them useful.
So consider what is in order to see the gain,
And consider what is not, to see its utility!

As we shall see from examples in the next chapter on Zhuangzi, the author of the *Dao-de Jing* is saying here that the spaces, whether in the centre of the hub, within the pot, or left for the windows and door, are not made by the artisan, and are therefore in accordance with Dao. The artisan is only making his structures 'conform' to the Dao, which is what gives the physical objects their utility.

It is easy to over-simplify this form of Daoism as back-to-nature escapism, but that would fail to do it justice. It is perhaps more an expressed form of opposition to the other ongoing strand of hierarchical thought, where life became highly formalised and relied upon such concepts as adherence to formal rites. These rites are reflected in the continuing production during the Western Zhou period of ritual vessels for offering food and drink to the ancestors or altars such as those to the earth or to the crops. To judge by the *Dao-de Jing*, the social structures and relationships of the administrators were anathema to Daoist thought, as shown by such sections as the highly ironic Section 18:

> When the great Dao is lost,
> Humaneness and Righteousness arise;
> When wisdom and intelligence emerge,
> The result is hypocrisy.
>
> When the six family relationships are forgotten,
> The result is filial piety;
> When the state is confused and chaotic
> Loyal ministers emerge.

As we shall see, Humaneness and Righteousness are fundamental virtues according to the tenets of Confucius, and filial piety and loyalty to one's superior in the hierarchy are also values that are an integral part of the Confucian theory. So, in Section 18, the writer is mocking these formal aspects of life, pointing out that such codified values are far inferior to the natural grain of things, which, if followed, will effortlessly bring good outcomes to those who follow it.

To summarise, we can say that the philosophy contained in the book *Laozi* is one in which all one's thoughts and actions should be carried out in conformity with the natural order of the world, contained within the concept of Dao, and that all action that would subvert this Dao will ultimately be ineffective. As far as the person Laozi is concerned, we cannot even be sure that he ever existed, but as we shall see in the next chapter, later Daoist texts provide plenty of anecdotes about him.

⊙ Chapter 4

The Teaching of Zhuangzi

Zhuangzi: the Man and the Book

As in the case of *Laozi*, the term *Zhuangzi* refers both to a man and to the book that bears his name. With Zhuangzi, however, we are much more certain about his actual existence and the time when he lived. Si-ma Qian refers to him in the *Shiji* – his name was Zhuang Zhou and he lived from around 369 to 286 BCE.

There is, however, no certainty about which parts of the *Zhuangzi* text were written by Zhuangzi himself. The earliest text of the *Zhuangzi* that we have is a compilation by the Daoist commentator Guo Xiang, who was writing in the third century CE, but scholars consider that the parts of the document relating to the third phase of Daoism (that is, following Yang Zhu and Laozi) probably represent authentic *Zhuangzi* material.

The advantage of reading the *Zhuangzi* text while studying Daoism is that, in contrast to the gnomic statements of the *Laozi*, it relies much more strongly on anecdotes, which can be considered under two main headings. The first concerns stories intended to illuminate the basic concepts of Daoism, while the second concerns anecdotes involving figures from other schools of philosophy and intended to highlight the superiority of Daoism over those schools. In the present chapter we shall look at some stories from the first of these two categories.

It is very clear from the text of the *Zhuangzi* that it stands in direct line of descent from the diviners and shamans. This is generally implicit in a number of the stories in the book, but we do have more concrete evidence that the *Zhuangzi* represents a continuation of these traditions.

In Chapter 26 of the book there is a story about a dream.

Lord Yuan of Song dreamed one night that a man covered in hair glanced in at the door, saying, 'I was on my way from the abyss of Cailu as an ambassador from the Qing River to the realm of the God of the Yellow River, but was caught by a fisherman, Yu Qie.'

Lord Yuan awoke and enquired of his councillors whether there was a fisherman called Yu Qie. Not only did he consult the diviners, who told him that the dream

was actually about a magic turtle, but on finding that Yu
Qie had actually caught a turtle five feet in circumference
it was decided to kill it and use its shell for divination.
The method of divination tallies exactly with the evidence
from the Shang oracle bones, being described as involving
the boring of seventy-two holes in the creature's shell,
'none of which yielded a false divination'.

In Chapter 14, the interpretation of a passage of
verse is offered with the introduction '*wu xian shao*
said'. The interpretation of the four Chinese characters
involved is not straightforward, since according to
Chinese dictionaries this name is the only occurrence of
the character *shao* (招), where it is explained as a name
of a minister, Wu Xian, of the Yin Dynasty, which was
the legendary precursor of the Shang. Looking up the
name Wu Xian, the dictionaries identify this individual
not only with the Yin Dynasty, but also with the time of
the legendary emperor Huangdi. From these references
the character *wu* (巫) in Wu Xian's name is highly
significant. The character was used to denote a shaman,
and in the references to Wu Xian the link to shamanism
is clear. For example, the *Liezi* says of Wu Xian that he
was a shaman of the time of Huangdi: 'There was a
shaman who came from Qi and settled in Zheng. His
name was Wu Xian. He understood the life and death,
existence and annihilation of Man, and the periods of
years, months, weeks and days, like a spirit.' Other
entries under this name simply say things like, 'Xian
was a shaman of the Yin'. On this evidence we can
conclude that the *Zhuangzi* is referring to a tradition
of shamanism believed to have originated in the
pre-Shang period.

Other stories in the *Zhuangzi*, however, have a much more direct bearing on our understanding of the *Laozi*. One of these is the story of a butcher who never needed to sharpen his knife:

Ding the butcher was cutting up an ox for Lord Hui of Wen. The movement of his hand, the attitude of his shoulder, the stance of his feet and the torsion of his knee, the sound of parting flesh, the sound of the blade, all blended as in the Dance of the Mulberry Grove, even as the chords of the Jing Shou. Lord Hui said, 'Excellent! How splendid that your skill has reached such an extent!'

Ding put away his knife and answered, 'What your servant loves is the Dao. It is more penetrating than skill. When your servant began first of all to cut up oxen, he could see nothing but the ox. After three years, I no longer tried to see the whole ox. Today, though, your servant engages through the spirit, rather than seeing with his eyes. Rational knowledge stalls, while the desire of the spirit carries forward. Relying upon the natural pattern, I strike the Dao's interstices and thus find the great cavities, in accordance with what is defined thereby. This same skill cleaves apart the joints, and more so the great bones.

'A good butcher changes his knife yearly. He cuts the meat. A lesser butcher changes his knife every month. He chops the meat. Today your servant's knife is nineteen years old, it has cut up a thousand oxen, but its edge is as if it has come

*fresh from the whetstone. The joints have natural
spaces within them, and the edge of my blade has
no thickness. I place the infinitely thin edge into
the natural space; is it not perfect how the
passage of the blade finds the requisite room!
This is why the edge of the blade maintains its
newly whetted condition after nineteen years.'*

Thus the intuition of the butcher in wielding his knife
so that it always follows the natural structure of the
ox's carcass permits the 'non-acting' blade to achieve
its result, as implied in the progression from the
'chopping' butcher who gets through twelve knives a
year, through the 'slicing' butcher whose knife lasts for
a whole year, to the Daoist perfection of Ding, whose
knife has butchered a thousand oxen yet appears
untouched.

One of the most famous stories in the *Zhuangzi* is
Zhuang Zhou's dream of the butterfly:

*Once upon a time, Zhuang Zhou dreamed that he
was a butterfly. He fluttered with joy as a
butterfly. He was so absorbed in this that he did
not know that he was Zhuang Zhou. Suddenly he
woke, and with a start was Zhou again. But he did
not know whether it was Zhou's dreaming of a
butterfly or the butterfly's dreaming of being
Zhou. But as between Zhou and the butterfly,
there must be a distinction. We call this the
changing of things.*

Despite its fame, and the fact that it deals with the mysterious nature of the mind and reality, the story does not fit immediately into the Daoism of the *Dao-de Jing*. In later centuries, however, this kind of Daoist idea would make it much easier for the followers of Buddhism in China to assert that Buddhism was a development of Daoism, aided by the legend that Laozi had travelled to India when he left 'through the Pass' (the Hangu Pass in the Western Mountains) and that Buddhism was based on his teaching.

Chapter 5

Confucius

The Need for Administration

We have seen how nature-based schools of thought, originating in the remotest times with shamanism and occultism, came to be the basis of the developing Daoist strand of Chinese philosophy. It was against this background that another strand of early Chinese society, the need to organise and manage the emerging city-states both individually and collectively, came into existence.

The rituals and ceremonies of the Shang and later dynasties, evidenced in the casting and inscribing of ceremonial bronze vessels, gradually evolved to provide a set of rites for the conduct of civil society. As we have discovered, the making of these ceremonial vessels continued from the Shang through the Western and the later, Eastern Zhou periods, and by this time the rites had become codified in the *Book of Rites* or, simply, 'the Rites', which was the handbook for behaviour at all levels in society. The change from Western to Eastern Zhou is marked by the end of central control by the Zhou clan. In the Eastern Zhou period, the rulers of individual states paid only lip-service to the rulers of the small State of Zhou, treating them as ceremonial monarchs whose task was to continue to conduct the Rites. The Eastern

Zhou period lasted from 722 to 403 BCE; after this date conflict between the Zhou states became the norm, and for this reason the time from 403 to 221 BCE is referred to as the Warring States period.

By the time of the Warring States period, the older pattern of control by punitive raids had changed. Now the individual states had standing armies that could be mobilised to secure and retain territory, and defended themselves by the construction of inter-state walls, many of which would later be linked up as components of the Qin Empire's 'Great Wall'.

To rule these states required organisation of the agricultural workforce, the craftsmen who provided the technologies of the day, the administrative class and the army. Something more than the Rites was needed to provide cohesion, and the most common 'glue' was provided by an appeal to the sage rulers of antiquity, as evidenced by the stories of the legendary kings and the folk memory of the Shang and Zhou periods.

The basis for evaluation of the past was contained in the so-called Five Classics. These were the *Book of Changes* (the *Zhou Li*), the *Book of Odes* (a collection of three hundred ancient poems), the *Book of History*, the *Rituals* (*Li*) and the *Spring and Autumn Annals* (a chronicle of the State of Lu from 722 to 479 BCE.

Confucius the Man

Into this situation came a man called Kong Zhongni. It is recorded by Si-ma Qian that Kong was born in the state of Lu in 552 or 551 BCE. He is said to have descended from an aristocratic family from Sung. One of his ancestors died when the heir of the Duke of Sung was assassinated while in his charge, and his family fled to the state of Lu. In the *Zuo Zhuan*, a commentary appended to the *Spring and Autumn Annals*, we find a reference to one Shu He, who held up a portcullis with his bare hands to enable the getaway to be made. A reference in the *Shiji* to apparently the same individual names him as Shu Lianghe and describes him as the father of Kong. Kong was to become a teacher, or *Zi*, and under the name Kongzi – 'Master Kong' – or Kong Fuzi he became known to the West as Confucius. His recorded sayings include the statement that he came from humble beginnings, hence his skill in menial things, and also that at the age of fifteen he set his heart on study, which in those days was the route to a career as an official.

Si-ma Qian records that Confucius became the police commissioner of Lu in the reign of Duke Ding of Lu (509–494 BCE). The *Zuo Zhuan* recounts how he accompanied the duke to a meeting with Duke Jing of Qi and scored a diplomatic victory. The *Zuo Zhuan* also records that Confucius was responsible for a failed plan to demolish the main city of each of the three most powerful noble families.

Confucius was obviously well versed in protocol. His departure from the state of Lu is recorded by the later writer of the book *Mengzi* (*Mencius*) in the following terms:

> *Mengzi said, 'Confucius was appointed justiciary official in the state of Lu, but his services were unused; attending the performance of a sacrifice the food offering was not proffered to him, and he left without even taking off his official headgear. Those who did not know [him] assumed that it was just because the food was not offered, while those who knew him felt that it was because of the improper performance of the Rites. But from Confucius' point of view, he preferred to leave because of this minor lapse of ritual, rather than departing for no reason.'*

Clearly Confucius was looking for an excuse to leave employment in the court of the ruler of Lu, and the failure of protocol gave him the chance to go, making an ethical statement at the same time by the manner of his departure. Nevertheless, the account in the *Mencius*, which is much closer to Confucius chronologically than Si-ma Qian and falls directly within the Confucian tradition, indicates not only that an under-employed Confucius was seeking an excuse to leave the service of the ruler of Lu, but further that the Rites were being followed in Lu, however imperfectly, and that lapses in the Rites were considered serious enough to be a plausible resigning matter for a state official.

Confucius left Lu in around 497 BCE and travelled to offer his advice to various of the Warring States. His first stop was in Wei, but he also visited Qi, Song, Chen and Cai. In none of these states did he achieve any success, and he returned home to Lu in 484 BCE at the age of sixty-eight to dedicate himself to teaching.

The *Analects* of Confucius

Although official record-keeping was well-established by the time of the Warring States, books were not produced by private individuals. Traditionally it used to be held that Confucius had either written, or at the least edited, some of the classic works which came to form the official canon of Confucianism, but scholars now generally agree that this was not the case. So, Confucius himself left no writings, whether of a public or a private nature. His students, many of whose names are known, passed on his teachings in turn to their students, and these, together with later generations of students, eventually compiled a collection of his words, the *Lun Yu* (論語), known in the West as the *Analects*. This is the work that gives us the most direct route to Confucius' teaching.

Having made his unsuccessful circuit of the courts of various of the Warring States, Confucius embarked on his late career as a teacher, and he concentrated on the idea of personal integrity, the character of the *junzi* (君子). Originally, this meant a prince or ruler, but in Confucianism it evolved into the meaning of 'the superior individual', in contrast to 'the petty man' (*xiao ren*, 小人).

What, then, were the characteristics of the superior individual as recorded in the *Analects*? That it was a key concept is clear from the outset of the book. The very first section of the first chapter reads as follows:

The Master [Confucius] said, 'If one studies with long practice, is this not enjoyable? If one is visited by distant friends, is this not a source of happiness? If one is not known, yet is not distressed by this, is this not the behaviour of the superior individual?'

In reading this saying, filtered through two or more generations of Confucian disciples, we can perhaps be forgiven for noting the aptness of this reference to the superior individual to Confucius' own failure to achieve success in his own time. Even so, the section not only underlines the role of the superior individual, but also reflects the high value the Confucians put on learning, as well as a focus on individual relationships through the concept of the superior individual.

In the next section, a second speaker, Youzi (Master You), says:

There are few whose character is that of a filial son, yet love to oppose their superiors! And there has never been a case of one who hates to oppose their superiors and yet loves to foment chaos. The superior individual concentrates on the basics. If the basics stand firm, the Dao [道] flourishes. Is not the filial son the basis of Ren [仁]?

This passage introduces three concepts that are key in the context of Confucianism. Let us first look at Dao. The character (道) is exactly the same as the one used by the Daoists as their key aspect. It still means 'the way' or 'the road', but in Confucian terms it has a different connotation from its Daoist usage. For the Confucian, the order which is desirable to be cultivated is the one underlying the basic stability of ordered human society, rather than the underlying structure of nature. Another fundamental commodity in Confucian theory is *ren* (仁). This is variously translated as 'humaneness', 'humanity' or 'human-heartedness', and relates to the way in which the individual behaves towards others. The third key concept in the passage is *xiao* (孝), filial piety, which should mark all relations of the inferior to his or her superior, whether this is a son/parent, subject/ruler or minister/monarch relationship. Only when all relationships are marked by an upwardly-directed *xiao* and a downwardly-directed *ren* will society be ordered according to the Confucian Dao.

Still in the first chapter of the *Analects*, the eighth section again refers to the superior individual:

> The Master said, 'If the superior man is not dignified, he will not instil awe, and his studies will not be firm. One whose words confirm integrity will not be burdened with friends who are not like this. If the superior individual acts wrongly, then he must not be afraid of putting it right.'

Here we are looking at an aspect of character which is related to what the Confucians regarded as another key component, namely *yi* (義), which can be translated as 'right conduct', although more usually rendered as 'righteousness'.

The final reference to the superior individual in the first chapter of the *Analects* is another reputed saying of Confucius:

The Master said, 'The superior individual is not greedy when he eats, nor in his dwelling does he crave tranquility. He is prompt in action and cautious in speech, so he possesses Dao and is confirmed by it, so we may say he loves study.'

The concept of *yi* is explicitly referred to in Section 13 of Chapter 1 of the *Analects*, where Youzi, again, is the speaker:

Youzi said, 'When good faith becomes right conduct, then words are fit to be repeated. When respect becomes expressed in Rites, disgrace is held at bay. Accordingly, one who does not neglect his parents, is also fit to be followed as a Master.'

This section introduces not only *yi*, right conduct, but *li* (禮), the Rites, as well, and draws on the concept of filial piety in the reference to the relationship of the individual to his parents.

The fourth of the Confucian virtues is *de* (德), normally translated as 'virtue', but which is more correctly viewed as an intrinsic 'force', 'essence' or 'power'. In Section 19 of Chapter 12 of the *Analects*, this usage of the character can be seen:

> *Ji Kang asked Confucius about government, 'What do you say about killing those who do not conform to Dao in order to advance those who do so conform?' Confucius replied, 'If you are governing, why do you employ killing? If you seek what is good, then the people will behave well, that's all. The essence of the superior individual is like the wind, that of the petty people is like the grass; if the wind blows over the grass, it must bend.'*

This last passage not only rounds off the four Confucian virtues; it also points to the way in which Confucius felt that his teaching was of relevance in government.

Who, then, should define and advise on such matters of conduct? Confucius' view was that this task should fall to the 'sage' (聖). He comments on the characteristics of a sage in Chapter 6 of the *Analects*:

> *Zi Gong said, 'What would you say of somebody who saves society by his generosity to ordinary people? Is it fitting to describe this as human-heartedness?' The Master [Confucius] said, 'How can you regard such behaviour as [merely] human-heartedness? What you have to understand is that this is the behaviour of a Sage. Consider Yao and Shun, were not they equally distressed?[1] Now, as far as human-heartedness goes, causing others to stand firm through one's*

own desire to stand firm, causing others to
develop through one's own desire to develop,
relying on one's inherent abilities in order to be an
example from which others may draw, may well
be called the pattern of human-heartedness.'

Translating Classical Chinese is a bit like describing a painting in words – there is never one 'correct' translation, and the original of this particular passage has been translated in different ways by different scholars. However, with the word 'merely' in parentheses and the footnote to the reference to Yao and Shun, the legendary Sage Kings, the present translation probably comes fairly close to reflecting Confucius' meaning in terms suitable for the general reader. Confucius is defining a sage as an individual in whom human-heartedness is developed to the highest degree. Indeed, the reference to Yao and Shun, with its echo of a legendary (and golden) antiquity, shows how much he felt that sages should be revered.

Confucius' concept of the sage is also significant because it points to the importance of the teacher, and hence of education. One of the marks of Confucianism as it developed in China was the role of the educated civil servant, who was trained in the Chinese Classics and qualified by rigorous examination.

We also have an example in the *Analects* of how Confucius actually looked at the practical aspect of government:

Zi Lu said, 'If the Duke of Wei delegated authority
to you, what would be your priority?'

Confucius said, 'My priority would be to rectify nomenclature.'
Zi Lu said: 'Is that it? You're way off the mark! Why rectify it?'
Confucius said, 'What a bumpkin! If there's something a superior man doesn't know, he keeps quiet. My argument is that if nomenclature is not rectified, then debate will be imprecise. If debate is imprecise, then appropriate results will not be achieved. If appropriate results are not achieved, then Rites and Music will not develop. If Rites and Music do not develop, then punishments will not fit crimes. If punishments do not fit crimes, then the populace will have no reliable guide for their actions. Therefore when a superior man uses a name, it must lead to correct speech, which in turn will lead to correct actions. So in his speech the superior man avoids all erroneous nomenclature.'

As we shall see, the 'Rectification of Names' was developed further by later philosophers.

We have seen in the *Analects* a package of attributes and attitudes which are of key significance to Confucianism. We will now look at how they formed a philosophy on which Chinese administration came to be based, at least in theory.

Confucianism in Government

How did the various ideas of Confucius combine to build a coherent philosophy? Confucius was looking for a society in which appropriate conduct by the individual would support an ordered framework of society. His was a hierarchical view of the world, built upon the idea that each individual in society owed a duty to his superiors and had responsibilities towards his inferiors. This two-fold relationship operated at all levels, so that the parent was responsible for his child, while the child owed filial obedience to the parent; the husband was responsible for his wife, while the wife owed a duty of obedience to her husband; the officials of state were responsible for the people, while the people owed a duty to the officials; and the ruler was responsible for the officials, while the officials owed a duty to the ruler. At the top of this hierarchical pyramid the ruler, frequently referred to as Tianzi (天子), 'the Son of Heaven', owed his position to Heaven. There is no formal religious significance to this phrase in Confucius' philosophy. The basic meaning of the character *tian* is the sky, and a frequent phrase for the world was *tianxia* (天下), which literally means 'all that is under the sky', so *tian* came to be understood as the ultimate framework for man's sphere of influence, and in Confucian thought there was still a need for the ruler to rule in accordance with the natural order of that framework. This later developed into the idea that the ruler only held power according to the 'Mandate of Tian'.

The secular nature of Confucius' philosophy, whatever his own personal views, is confirmed by a well-known story from the *Analects* (11.12):

When Qi Lu asked about serving ghosts and spirits, the Master replied, 'If you have not yet developed the ability to serve people, how are you able to serve ghosts and spirits?' and when he ventured to

*ask about death, the reply was, 'If you have not yet
developed an understanding of life, how can you
understand death?'*

So we arrive at a philosophy of society and
administration that is based upon a web of
relationships, characterised by human-heartedness and
righteousness, and conducted in conformity to an over-
arching pattern, or Dao. The philosophy is underpinned
by the precepts contained in the Chinese Classics, as
interpreted by Confucius and later sages, where virtue
and human-heartedness are of the highest order, and
by an educational process through which, in particular,
the administrators of a kingdom become qualified to
conduct their profession.

It is fair to say that even before the time of
Confucius there was an educated and literate class in
China. Written books were in existence from at least
the Spring and Autumn period, and by Confucius' time
there was a body of books which were held to contain
information and guidance. Record-keeping by the
various kingdoms was established, so there was to
some extent a bureaucracy, but when the relative
order of the Spring and Autumn states collapsed and
spawned the turbulence of the Warring States period,
many, Confucius included, felt that only by a
thoroughgoing renewal of the principles of
administration could the rulers re-establish an age
of stability and good governance. It was this impulse
which led Confucius to make his tour of the
neighbouring states, and then, when his advice had

been overlooked, to embark upon his career as a teacher.

As an administrative reformer, Confucius clearly failed, but as a teacher and sage his recorded sayings in the *Lun Yu* were to form a springboard from which later generations of Confucian philosophers and teachers would launch the theoretical underpinning of Chinese government administration for centuries to come.

Chapter 6

Mozi, the First Opponent of Confucius

The Point at Issue

One feature of the web of relationships proposed by Confucius is that the strength of the bonds depend on the distance between the parties, so that in the hierarchical pyramid, the greater the distance either across a single layer or between different layers, the less strong the degree of duty and responsibility becomes. Thus one's immediate family members demand stronger ties than do remoter relations, and family ties are stronger than the ties of friendship. This was to become a key point of difference between the Confucian school of philosophy and its first serious rival.

Mozi's Background

The founder of this rival school of thought was a man called Mo Di, who lived from *c.* 479 to *c.* 381 BCE. Like Confucius, he became known as a 'teacher' or 'master' – Mozi. While Confucius' thought was based on the historic traditions of the Zhou dynasty, stressing the value of rituals, music and literature, and developing from them his ethical framework of civilised existence, Mo Di was more of a reformer, focusing on the deficiencies of the existing order and proposing radical change. Each, of course, was looking at ways of addressing the increasingly chaotic situation in the Warring States period, but while Confucius approached the problem from the standpoint of a scholar-sage, Mo Di came from a military background, and launched his fierce criticism of both the ancient traditions and Confucius' thought from a pragmatic point of view.

Both the scholars and the military men (sometimes known as *xie* (侠), or 'knights-errant') had their origins as specialists in the courts of the rulers of the Chou period, but as the regime collapsed, they lost their official positions and offered their services to anyone who was willing to employ them. We have seen how Confucius fell into this role, and we can find out about the development of the knights-errant from the 'Treatise on the Knights-errant' in Chapter 124 of the *Shiji* of Si-ma Qian. First Si-ma Qian quotes Han Fei, a Legalist philosopher whom we shall meet later and who takes a jaundiced view of both the scholars and the knights-errant, as follows: 'The scholars threw law into chaos by their literature, the military men opposed restrictions by feats of arms.'

To this Si-ma Qian adds a comment that each of the two groups can be criticised, and both scholars and warriors have been weighed by the opinions of the world. After a brief discussion of the knights-errant of the Spring and Autumn period, he then goes on to talk about how they were viewed in his own time:

> By contrast, the conduct of the knights-errant today is not as traitors to the right conduct of government; but still, their words are to be believed, their conduct is fruitful, what they agree to is true. They do not love their physical self, they hasten to relieve the troops' difficult distress; having withstood events involving existence and destruction, death and life, they do not boast of their abilities, and are diffident to boast of their virtue.

This, then, was the background from which Mo Di came, and it is no surprise that he approached life from a military point of view. Nine chapters of the book that bears his name are concerned with the fortification and defence of towns, and he is said to have had nearly two hundred disciples, all of whom would, on his orders, enter flames or walk on swords, not turning back in the face of death. The training Mo Di offered was intended to produce different knights-errant from those criticised by Han Fei. However, it is clear that his underlying ethos is in stark contrast to that of Confucius, which Mo Di opposed through his distinct philosophy.

Mo Di's Arguments

- The failure of Confucianism to take account of gods and spirits displeases these entities, and so the Confucian system of government must be inauspicious.
- The Confucians waste resources and energy in elaborate funerals and the formal three-year mourning period that they prescribe for the death of a parent.

> *Today the funeral rites for kings, dukes and grandees are quite different [from those practised by the Sage Kings Yao, Shun and Yu the Great]. There is inevitably both an outer and an inner coffin, three layers of leather or silk outer wrapping, jade and jadeite artefacts, and various bronze items – lances, swords, ding vessels, drums, pots and jugs. (Mozi 6.3)*
> (These practices are fully corroborated by recent archaeological evidence from China.)

- The Confucians are obsessed with the practice of music, which also wastes resources and energy in useless activities.
- The Confucians are fatalists, which leads to laziness among the people, who resign themselves to fate rather than acting to improve their lot.

Elsewhere in the book, in a chapter explicitly entitled 'Opposing Confucianism', Mo Di rails against the length of time expended in the basic Confucian education, the excessive – and unproductive – burden of performance of ceremonial duties, the crippling expense of providing music in the Confucian manner, and finally the seduction of the ruler by the 'enhanced beauty of wicked arts'. These shortcomings, says Mo Di, mean that Confucianism cannot meet the needs of the age, nor can it effectively educate the people.

We can see in these objections the attitudes that Confucius and Mo Di brought from their different backgrounds, the scholar and the military man respectively. Both were seeking a rationale for a better way of government, and perhaps the chronological separation between them led Mo Di, who lived later in the period of conflict which characterised the Warring States, towards a philosophically based, but still military, solution.

Hierarchy versus universal love

Mo Di did not altogether reject the Confucian ideas of *ren* and *yi*, but he insisted that they were universal and constant, rather than hierarchical. This is a direct result of Mo Di's military background, for the ethos of the knights-errant could be expressed as, 'All for one and one for all'. All knights-errant should 'enjoy equally and suffer equally' according to Mo Di, who reasoned that everyone in the world should love everyone else equally. He distinguished this from a Confucianism in which there was discrimination in the degree of love between, for example, relatives and friends. On this basis, argued Mo Di, friends will come off second best under Confucianism, whereas in Mo Di's system, one should do one's utmost to care for one's friends.

Mo Di relied on three tests to evaluate philosophical principles:

- Is this based on the Will of Heaven, the will of the spirits and the actions of the ancient Sage Kings?
- Is it compatible with the view of the common people?
- When applied in government, does it benefit the state and the people?

Mo Di regarded the last of these tests as the most important, and when applying it in order to discriminate between universal love and hierarchical, graded love, he came to the conclusion that since the task of the human-hearted man is to facilitate the well-being of the world and to remove its disasters, the causes of the disasters themselves are the root of the problem. He argues that the acts of oppression of powerful states against the weaker states, of powerful aristocratic families against the less powerful ones, and of more powerful or devious individuals against their victims, can all be seen to arise because the strong act with hatred towards the weak. Confucianism, with its idea of graded love, accentuates this oppression and is therefore undesirable. Mo Di's universal love, he asserts, will do away with these disasters of society, and lead to an ideal world in which the human-hearted man can rule a state to the benefit of all its members.

As we shall see, some of the pragmatic aspects of Mohism (the philosophy of Mozi) would recur in the thoughts of the Legalists, but the concept of universal love, his main point of departure from Confucianism, would not be one of them.

Chapter 7

Mencius, Exponent of Confucius' Ideas

Mencius the Man

Mo Di's life was sandwiched between the death of Confucius and the birth of Mencius, who was Confucius' most significant early interpreter and is said to have studied Confucian doctrine under a disciple of Zi Si, who was Confucius' grandson.

Mencius is a Latinised form of the Chinese name Mengzi, 'Master Meng', and in this chapter we shall refer to the individual as Mencius and the book about his life and teaching as the *Mengzi*.

The earliest account of Mencius' life is to be found in the *Shiji* of Si-ma Qian, where he is stated to have been from the state of Zou, from where he began his travels to converse with various rulers on the matter of

government. He first secured official status in around 320 BCE under King Hui of Liang, but subsequently found problems in getting his ideas accepted because, as Si-ma Qian records, the Warring States had entered a phase of major inter-state alliances, and their concentration on military and security affairs meant that Mencius' teaching of the Sage

Kings and Confucius' philosophy was largely irrelevant to the turbulent environment. The extent of militarisation at this time can be gauged from the reference made by Si-ma Qian to the employment of Sunzi, author of the still authoritative book *The Art of War*, to assist the state of Qi in obtaining the subjection of the feudal lords to its rule. As in the case of Confucius, the disappointed philosopher retired to teach, and his disciples, possibly with the participation of Mencius himself, set down his teaching in the book that bears his name, the *Mengzi*.

The Book of Mencius

The *Mengzi* is a compilation of stories about Mencius, his disciples and his teaching, and is a rich source of information about Confucianism in the fifth century BCE. Because of its directly anecdotal nature, it is far easier to follow than the *Analects* of Confucius, and because of its authorship, even if Mencius' own authorship is imaginary, it is much closer in time to Mencius than is the *Analects* to Confucius. The stories in the *Mengzi* also relate to individuals who are known from other historical records and traditions, so we get a very clear impression of Mencius' times and the key elements of Confucian philosophy of the period.

The Goodness of Human Nature

One of Mencius' main projects in philosophy was to close a gap in the Confucian account of humanity. In all his recorded sayings, Confucius never presented an argument about why it was that a man should act in accordance with *yi*, righteous conduct, and practice *ren*, human-heartedness. Mencius made it one of his aims to explain this principle, and in so doing he explored the quality of human nature.

According to Mencius, this question had previously been given three possibilities:

- That human nature is neither good nor bad, as proposed by his contemporary, Gaozi.
- That human nature is either good or bad.
- That the nature of some men is good, and of other men is bad.

In Mencius' opinion these views were all in error. He taught that human nature was inherently good, and that other elements, which although not inherently bad might lead to bad results, were those that mankind held in common with the animal kingdom, and so were not strictly part of human nature. Therefore, concluded Mencius, *human* nature could be seen as inherently good. The *Mengzi* expresses this as follows:

Mencius said, 'All men by nature have a kind[2] heart. The kings of antiquity had kind hearts, and so their government was kind. By applying a kind heart to practice kind government, in administering the whole

world one may turn it in the palm of one's hand.
'It follows from the proposition that all men have
a kind heart, that if now anyone suddenly were to
see an infant about to fall into a well, they would
react with alarm and distress. This is not because
they seek praise from the child's parents, nor is it
because they wish to gain the praise of their
neighbours and friends, nor because they fear
for their reputation should they not intervene in
the situation.

'From this we can see one who lacks compassion is
not fully human, one who fails to abhor evil is not fully
human, one who lacks modesty is not fully human,
one who lacks a conscience[3] is not fully human.
Compassion is the origin of Ren, abhorrence of evil is
the origin of right conduct, modesty is the origin of
ritual and conscience is the origin of wisdom.'

From this conclusion, Mencius then proceeds
to the proposition that it is the duty of mankind
to develop these four characteristics – *ren* (仁),
yi (義), *li* (禮) and *zhi* (智) – to become a
fully developed human being. From this it follows
that education in the Confucian manner is a matter
of guiding the goodness inherent in human nature. In
this way Mencius uses a single parable to tie together
ren, *yi*, *li* and *zhi* in a coherent scheme. This was to
become the dominant theme of Confucianism through
the ages, and survived despite efforts by later Confucian
thinkers to overturn Mencius' idea of the inherent
goodness of mankind.

The Mandate of Heaven

In addition to Mencius' innovation in declaring this innate goodness, the *Mengzi* also expands and clarifies the basic ideas referred to in Confucius' *Analects*. A key idea in this category is the Mandate of Heaven (天命, *tian ming*), deriving from a very early idea in Chinese philosophy, probably current among the early occultists. There had long been a theory that Man's activities were conducted under a generally benign influence of *tian*, which literally means 'sky', and had extended connotations similar to the Western word 'heaven', although the Chinese *tian* is perhaps more of a power base than a mystical paradise. We first come across the phrase *tian ming* in the *Book of Documents* (*Shu Jing*), sometimes referred to as the *Book of History*.

The *Shu Jing* is a collection of documents referring to very ancient events, from the earliest times down to the Zhou Dynasty, which was believed to have been either written or edited by Confucius. This gave it an exalted status among the Confucians and others, and it formed a valued source of historical information for later generations of Chinese scholars and administrators. We now know that Confucius probably had nothing to do with its compilation, and that much of its material dates from the third century BCE, although stylistic grounds indicate that it contains material from very early times. Other material is almost certainly an imaginative re-creation of the third century BCE or thereabouts, and one such passage is 'the Proclamation of Tang', which purports to be the inaugural speech of the first ruler of the Shang Dynasty.

In the Proclamation, Tang has returned from the conquest of Xia to great acclaim, and addresses 'the populace from all the ten thousand directions'. He invokes 'the August Emperor of Tian' as the one who sends down righteousness upon the people of the earth. If, he says, one has a constant nature, then one can restrain one's discourse and consider one's successors. However, the king of Xia had extinguished virtue and practised oppression, visiting great calamity on those who now made up his audience, and dragging them into his cruelty so that they could not endure the consequences and shouted in protest to spirits both high and low. Since Tian's way is to reward the good and punish evil, calamity fell upon Xia as punishment for its crimes. Tang continues:

Then, taking the bright majesty of the Mandate of Heaven, I did not dare to grant pardon. I presumed to use a dark-coloured male sacrifice,[4] and to call on the spirits of highest Tian, requesting that Xia be punished. Then I sought the primal Sage and joined my strength with his so that together with you all I should request the Mandate. Highest Tian confirmed its blessing of the people, and the criminal has been crushed. The Mandate of Heaven did not err in this; embellished like the grasses and trees, the augury showed that the people will grow in trust.[5]

This passage, taken from one of the Confucian Classics, clearly shows how a ruler was considered to rule only so long as he had Tian's authority to do so. Should he fail to rule well, Tian would withdraw the mandate from the present ruler and grant it instead to the leader of the successor regime. This had two long-term consequences for government administration in China. First, successful rebellion was philosophically and politically viewed as legitimate, so the administration of the state could continue uninterrupted, often with the same civil service in place. Secondly, because the succession of regimes was built into the conceptual system of the administrators, each regime from the Han onward was to have an Office of History that would compile an archive of material specifically for use by the successor regime to write the history of its predecessor.

This explanation puts into perspective the brief reference to the Mandate of Heaven in the *Analects*, where Confucius is recorded as saying:

*At fifteen my mind was set on study, by thirty
I was established, by forty I had no doubts, at fifty
I understood the Mandate of Heaven, at sixty I
understood all I heard, at seventy I followed my
heart's wishes, without offending.*

Confucius clearly felt that the Mandate of Heaven was something one only understood after considerable study, which would have involved the study of the *Book of Documents* and the *Book of Odes*. The latter, as we have seen, was another of the Confucian Classics, and is a collection of ancient verse. Mencius refers to it in the one chapter of the *Mengzi* where he uses the phrase 天命, *tian ming*:

> Mencius said, 'If the world is characterised by Dao, those of lesser virtue will serve those of greater virtue, and those of lesser wisdom will serve those of greater wisdom, whereas if the world lacks Dao, the small serve the great and the weak serve the strong. These two cases are a consequence of Tian. Those who follow Tian survive, but those who rebel against Tian are lost. Duke Jing of Qi said, "Since we cannot successfully command, neither can we receive the Mandate; this means that we are finished." Weeping, he sent his womenfolk to the state of Wu.[6] Today small states emulate large states, but are ashamed at receiving their orders, but this is like a small boy being ashamed at taking instruction from his teacher. If one is ashamed like this, none is more worth emulating than King Wen. By emulating King Wen, a large state could extend its rule to the whole world within five years, a small state within seven years. The Book of Odes says:

> "The descendants of Shang
> numbered not less than one hundred thousand,
> Shangdi terminated the Mandate,
> they were bound in subjection to Zhou.
> Subjected to Zhou
> because Tian's Mandate is not unchanging.
> The knights of Yin are fine active men,
> but they poured their libations in the capital
> of Zhou."

Confucius said, "Ren cannot be achieved by
numbers. However, consider when the ruler loves
Ren, his realm will have no enemies." Today, to wish
to have no enemies in the realm, while not using Ren,
is like grasping fire before quenching it. The Book of
Odes says,

> *"Who is able to grasp the flame*
> *without even thinking of quenching it?"'*

This passage, with its references to Confucius and the
Book of Odes, makes it clear where Mencius stands on
the question of the Mandate of Heaven. He also makes
many references to Tian as an entity which influences
the destiny of rulers and states, and in this way he
established the doctrine of the Mandate of Heaven as a
cornerstone of Confucianism.

Government

Having secured the Mandate of Heaven, how then
should the ruler maintain it? Mencius confirms very
clearly that the well-being of the state is based on
Confucius' idea of a series of hierarchical relationships,
and he gives a number of examples which flesh out the
brief statements in the *Analects*.

One of his conversations with Duke Xuan of Qi, who
asked him about governing his state, concluded with
the following:

If you wish to practice it, then why do you not
return to its fundamentals? If a plot of 5 mu were
planted up with mulberry trees,[7] then people of

fifty may be clothed in silk. If the husbandry of chickens, pigs, dogs and boar is well-conducted, then people of seventy may eat meat. If you do not snatch away cultivation time from 100 mu of arable land, then a household of eight people will avoid starvation. If you supervise what is taught in the schools, and ensure that it will teach fraternal right-conduct, then those whose hair is streaked with white will not carry burdens on the road. There has never been a failure of rule when the old are well-dressed and well-fed and the populace is free from hunger and calamity.

So, in Mencius' view, the basis of good government demands physical and mental well-being among the people, and the foundation of the latter is a sound education in filial duty. The reference to cultivation time being 'snatched away' from the land in this passage refers to the tendency of landowners to demand service from agricultural workers, who could not then tend their own crops. In Confucian theory, land tenure and duty to the landowner were described in terms of what was known as the 'well field' system (井田). The shape of the character for a well (井) divides a roughly square area into nine equal sub-areas, and in the following passage the descriptions of areas and sub-areas are based on this pattern, referred to as a 'well'. It is unlikely that the areas discussed actually constituted a neat 'well' pattern, but rather that the 'well' analogy neatly defined an 8:1 ratio:

Bi Zhan of Teng was sent to ask about dividing land according to the well pattern.

Mencius said, 'Your ruler wants to conduct human-hearted government, and he selected you as his ambassador, so you must be worthy of your insignia of office.

'Now, as to human-hearted government, it must originate in the fixing of boundaries. If the boundaries are not correctly fixed, the well pattern will not be regular, and the yield of crops will not be even, which is why harsh rulers and vile ministers [8] *are lax in fixing boundaries. If boundaries are fixed correctly, then both the areas and the yields can be determined in accordance with rank.*

'Now, as to the state of Teng, its territory is limited, but there must be a ruler there, and there must be people. If there were no ruler, there would be nobody to govern the people, while if there were no people, there would be nobody to provide for the ruler's needs. I would respectfully suggest that in the country there be a labour obligation of one ninth, while in the city [9] *there be a tax levy of one tenth. Ministers of state and below would have land to support their ritual sacrifices, this land to be 50 mu in area. Additional able-bodied men should be allocated 25 mu. Neither funerals nor changes of address shall pass outside the village boundaries. The village land shall be in a well pattern, and if those with business there enjoy mutual friendship, are vigilant in mutual*

*support and help each other in times of sickness,
then the people will coalesce in harmony.*

'The well pattern should be one li square,[10]
*giving a total area of 900 mu. The central area
should be the common field, and eight households
should each have a private area of 100 mu. They
should work together to cultivate the common
field, and when the common work is completed,
they should be at liberty to begin their private
work. This is how people living in the country
would make their contribution, as distinct from
the others.*

*'This is a broad summary of the idea; if you wish to
elaborate it, then it is for your ruler and yourself to do.'*

This explanation of the well field system by Mencius
establishes that land allocation is at the heart of an
administration conducted according to ren. He explicitly
criticises the unfair distributions that have taken place
to line the pockets of officials and sets out a formalised
system in which in rural areas the population can have
an allocation of land within strictly defined terms, but
the local grandee is supported by the produce of the
common field at the centre of the well field pattern and
has priority over the labour of the villagers, who have to
work the common field before working on their own. The
village is seen as a self-contained and self-perpetuating
unit, and would form the background to the situation
set out in the previous passage. One implication of the
passage is that the capital city of the state, where the

distinctive form of rural agricultural service was not required, was a city of traders and artisans who were not involved in agriculture but worked in a money economy and could buy in agricultural produce. This is consistent with the early rise of copper currency in China. Archaeologists date this from at least as far back as the eighth century BCE.

Mencius' Rebuttal of Mozi

One thing which is clear from the *Mengzi* is the need for mutual regard and support, and as we have seen, Mozi had already diverged from Confucius' view of graded love. Mencius favoured the Confucian rather than the Mohist line on this question, and he is recorded in the *Mengzi* as specifically opposing Mozi's theory:

> [Mencius said:] '... there have been no Sage Kings [since the time of the Spring and Autumn Annals]. The feudal lords are wildly unconstrained, the unattached officers express themselves perversely, Yang Zhu and Mo Di's words fill up the world. If the words of the world do not follow Yang, then they follow Mo. The followers of Yang serve themselves; this is to remove the role of one's ruler. The followers of Mo love in an all-embracing manner; this is to remove the role of one's father. To act as if there were no ruler or parent is the way of animals. ... If the Dao of Yang and Mo does not cease, and the Dao of Confucius is not proclaimed, the people will be deceived by depraved teaching, and so human-heartedness and righteous conduct will be

completely suppressed. If this were to happen, then the people would be consumed by the encouragement of animal behaviour, and the people would consume each other. Because I am afraid of this, I guard the Dao of the former sages, distance myself from Yang and Mo, and refute licentious teachings, so that these heretics will not prevail. If their thought were to prevail, it would be carried out through their actions, and if their actions were to prevail, this would destroy government. Were another sage to arise, he would not vary my words.'

Mencius' strength of feeling is very clear from this passage, his support of traditional Confucian and sagely attitudes is very explicit, and he further cites the examples of Yu the Great and the Duke of Zhou in dealing with rebellious subjects and unfilial sons. Yet in aligning himself with these worthy figures, he remains self-deprecating:

How could anyone claim that I like disputing? But I cannot manage to avoid it. One who can by his words oppose Yang and Mo is a true follower of the Sages.

Mencius' appeal, in this and other passages in the *Mengzi*, to the traditional values of Confucianism backed by the examples of the earlier sages and Sage Kings, both real and legendary, was to provide a platform for all later strands of Confucian philosophy, despite various attempts to introduce modifications.

Chapter 8

Xünzi, Critic
of Mencius

Xünzi the Man

Mencius' strong support for traditional Confucian
philosophy and vehement opposition to the views of the
Mohist interpretations were not accepted by all. The
earliest opponent whose writings survive was Xünzi,
whose name, 'Master Xün', like Mozi and Mencius
before him, refers to both the man and his writings. To
distinguish the man and his book, we shall refer to Xünzi
the philosopher as Xün, and to the book as the *Xünzi*.

Xün is referred to in Si-ma Qian's *Shiji*. His actual
name was Xün Kuang or Xün Qing, and he came from
the state of Zhao. He followed the pattern of previous
Confucian philosophers, in that when he was fifty years
old he travelled to the state of Qi and played a
prominent role in the Jixia Academy, which was a major
centre of learning. This did not, of course, guarantee
that his ideas would be practised by either Zhao or Qi,
since the headlong destruction of the Warring States
continued to accelerate, and pragmatism was more
valuable than abstract philosophy.

To judge from his writings Xün was primarily
concerned with human ethics, which he viewed as a
somewhat separate matter from the affairs of Heaven
or the World. Thus he deals in some detail with matters

of human culture, which he sees as self-sufficient, albeit on a stage in which Heaven and Earth are an integral part of the scenery.  Mainstream Confucianism, as we have seen, paid specific regard particularly to the relationship between Man (particularly the Superior Man or ruler) and Tian, or Heaven. This difference in approach leads Xün to specific points of difference from mainstream Confucianism, as we shall see when we look in more detail at the *Xünzi*.

The Book of Xünzi

In contrast to the earlier writings carrying the names of Confucius and Mencius, it is believed that Xün Kuang himself wrote much of the contents of the *Xünzi*, so we have a much more direct route into his thinking than we do into that of his predecessors.

The style of the book is much more systematically argued than the more anecdotal and personal *Mengzi*, and it sets out to present logical arguments for its propositions.

It is generally held that the main difference between Xün and Mencius is that while Mencius argued that the nature of mankind is inherently good, Xün considered that it was inherently evil but amenable to improvement by education. This, however, is a consequence of Xün's underlying thought, which can be seen from a passage in Chapter 17 of the *Xünzi*, where Xün is describing the nature of the tripartite division of Heaven, Earth and Mankind:

> *Tian is characterised by its seasons. Di [地, the Earth] is characterised by its wealth of resources. Mankind is characterised by its powers of organisation; this is what we call being able to be a member of the Three.*

Later in the same chapter, Xün discusses how the affairs of Tian, Di and mankind are separate, and in Confucian manner calls on the *Book of Odes* to give him suitable back-up:

The Book of Odes says:

> *'Tian made the high mountain,*
> *The great King brought it under cultivation*
> *That was its beginning.*
> *King Wen made it prosper'*

That is what we mean by it.

By citing this poem, Xün is linking the roles of Tian in creating the mountain, Di in providing the plants which might be cultivated and mankind in having the applied skill to work with the materials provided by Tian and Di.

Human nature as evil

Because mankind had no interactive relationship with Tian or Di, Xün held that mankind had no inbuilt moral/ethical basis, and that therefore this aspect of humanity had to be inculcated by education. In contrast to Mencius' homely parable of the child about to topple into a well, Chapter 23 of the *Xünzi* opens uncompromisingly:

Human nature is evil. Any goodness is spurious. Nowadays the nature of mankind from birth is to acquire a love of profit, and following from this love, rapacity flourishes and courtesy is swept away. From birth, mankind is incorrigibly evil, and following from this evil nature, vicious homicides flourish and loyal sincerity is swept away. From birth, mankind enjoys the senses of sight and sound, and is seduced by sounds and colours, and from this seduction immoral disorder flourishes, and Rites and righteous conduct are swept away. This being the case, then to follow human nature and human feelings always results in rapacity combined with opposition to duty and overthrowing of order, and so a descent into violence.

Therefore it is essential to adopt a transformation by teaching law, and the Dao of Rites and righteous conduct. If this is done, then the consequence will be the emergence of courtesy combined with order, and a return to true governance.

Having established this theory, Xün later in the same chapter of the *Xünzi* takes as vigorous a view of Mencius' theory of innate human goodness as Mencius before him had taken of the philosophical line of Yang Zhu and Mo Di:

Mencius said that human nature is good. I say that this is not so. Universally and through all ages, that which has been called 'good' is right ordering and peaceful government, while that which has been called 'evil' is corruption and chaos. This is the distinction between good and evil. Following Mencius, the goodness of Man would result in right ordering and peaceful government, but that would imply that the Sage Kings on the one hand and Rites and right conduct on the other were the tools of evil [because their control was directed against inherent goodness], and then how could they foster right ordering and peaceful government? Now, since this is not the case, I conclude that it is human nature that is evil.

This approach to human nature, although it was destined to fall out of favour with later Confucian philosophers, would, as we shall see, find supporters among the so-called Legalists of later centuries, and so had a significant influence on the broader canvas of Chinese philosophy.

The nature of human society

Another consequence of human nature that concerned Xün was the way in which human society operated. By his time the specialisation of artisans in towns and cities was very well established, so, as we have already seen, different sections of the population depended upon each other's labour to secure the means of subsistence. His view of human nature led him to believe that two extremes of behaviour would each lead to problems. In Chapter 10 of the *Xünzi*, he says:

> [People] have the same desires and hates, but their desires are many and things are few. Their scarcity inevitably leads to conflict. For this reason the products of a hundred artisans are the means by which one individual is maintained, but the skilled artisan cannot practise two skills at the same time. Nor can anybody hold two offices of state. If people live apart and do not co-operate then the result will be poverty, while if they form a disorganised mob, there will be conflict.

Xün's answer to this situation was two-fold. In the first place, he argued, it was necessary for there to be an ordered society, so that resources could be efficiently shared among the people, and in the second place, an ordered society could only arise and be maintained if the Rites and righteous behaviour were taught, in which case the human power of reasoning, rather than any innate goodness in human beings, would enable society to be well regulated.

A Pragmatic Approach to the Rites and Music

Xün's approach to the Rites was pragmatic rather than mystical. For example, his attitude to funerary rites was that they served to mark one's respect for human life and, in particular, for the life of the deceased.

Therefore I say, the sacrifices are inspired by affectionate ideas and thoughtful regard, the outcome of piety and loving respect, the height of propriety and refinement. I, Xün, am not a Sage, so I cannot comprehend them. The Sage comprehends them clearly, skilled rulers follow them effortlessly, lesser officials value them, and the populace at large accept them as their customs. They are regarded by rulers as man-made, but the people regard them as a matter of spirits.

He felt similarly about music, which Confucians regarded as necessary to the regulation of the state, but which, in Xün's view, was more a question of individual appreciation rather than being an integral part of administration. His view, similar to his view of the Rites, is expressed as:

Therefore I say this as far as the appreciation of music is concerned. The ruler establishes his Dao by music; petty men satisfy their desires by music.

The Importance of Correct Definitions

Xün is also concerned with another of the recurring topics of Confucianism that we have encountered – the question of correct naming of things. As we shall see in the next chapter, this may in fact have arisen because of the use of the character script which had evolved in China over time, but it was clearly felt that for good administration the name of a thing had to correspond to the reality. Xün devotes a complete chapter of the *Xünzi* to this topic, and early in the chapter he says:

> *Should one arise who has the attributes of a true king, he will inevitably be one who conforms to ancient names, and is active in making new names . . . . Therefore when one who is a true king has instituted a name, the corresponding reality is distinct. His will can be put into effect because the Dao has been followed and so by his careful lead he unites the populace at large.*

Xün believed that failure to control the application of names would lead to utter confusion:

> *Therefore to fragment the language and coin names unilaterally, thereby confusing the regular names, is to cause deception of the populace.*

People will argue about the distinctions [between names], which could be described as a great treason. This crime is as bad as the crime of giving false measure.

Xün's views on the correct handling of names led him to oppose the arguments of what we know as the philosophical 'School of Names' just as vehemently as he opposed Mencius' view of human nature and the role of Tian in the affairs of the state. We shall see why this was so in the next chapter.

Xünzi's Influence on Philosophy

In many ways Xün seems to have provided a 'reformed' Confucianism, in which the influences of spiritual forces were demoted and the Confucian view was explained in terms of human behaviour. However, his thought included the idea that ideal rule would come into being if a Sage King were to ascend to the throne, and the people were educated to apply their reason to life so that they would obey the rule of the Sage King and form an ordered society in which individuals co-operated in the interest of the common good. In a time of increasing political and military conflict, Xün felt that only in such circumstances could the whole of China be united under an acceptable administration.

Xün's version of Confucian philosophy had short- and medium-term influence, but in the longer term the reputation of his immediate followers undermined its survival. The unification of China under a single ruler would be achieved in 221 BCE, and two individuals, Li Si and Han Fei, who took Xün's teaching to heart, were instrumental in this result. They established a new school of philosophy, Legalism (see chapter 10), whose discipline and cruelty were so extreme that although it served as the political engine of unification under the Qin, it also led to the downfall of that dynasty in a very short space of time. The Legalist philosophical strand was thus discredited and a more conservative form of Confucianism would arise, based largely on the ideas of Confucius and Mencius and ignoring those aspects on which the Legalists had based their administrative ideas.

⊙ Chapter 9

The School of Names

The Need to Define Things

The 'Rectification of Names' was, as we have seen, one of the long-standing topics of Confucian philosophy. From Confucius, through Mo Di and Mencius, and on to Xunzi, the matching of name to reality was considered to be one of the most important matters in administering a state. Its level of importance can be judged by the fact that there was a group of philosophers whose attention was focused on the matter of naming, who are collectively referred to as 'the School of Names' – although another name which was applied to them is 'the Arguers'.

The School of Names frequently expressed its thoughts by using paradoxical statements which showed how necessary it was not only to know the relationship between a name and the corresponding reality, but also to appreciate how context was vital in determining what a sentence meant. For example, Hui Shi (*c.* 350–260 BCE) is quoted in the *Zhuangzi* as saying such things as, 'The sky is as low as the earth; the mountains are on the same level as marshes', by which he meant that in each case the impression you get depends on where you are standing in relation to the two things: the sky, however high it may extend, meets the earth at the horizon, and marshes may be found in the upper reaches of mountains.

Hui Shi also extended his approach to more abstract concepts, saying for example that 'the greatest has nothing beyond itself and is called "Great One". The smallest has nothing within it and is called "Small one".' These postulates are intended to set maximum and minimum limits to the conceptual understanding of the physical world irrespective of the size of any particular thing in the world, and in so doing introduce the concept that there must be both something ultimately large and something ultimately small.

Gong-sun Long and the White Horse Debate

Perhaps the best-known philosopher of the School of Names was Gong-sun Long, the author of a book bearing his name and containing one of the most famous paradoxes of all time. This is the 'White Horse' debate, and it is very interesting in the light it casts on Chinese language and its writing system, since precision of

language and its implications for philosophy and legal systems were of great importance to the Chinese themselves. The White Horse debate, which is written as if taking place between two people, begins:

A white horse is not a horse; what's your view about that?

Unfortunately, when Western scholars first tried to understand Gong-sun Long's arguments, they noted that the School of Names was roughly contemporary with the Greek philosophers who discussed logic in terms of paradoxes, and assumed that the School of Names was involved in similar arguments. From this basis they found great difficulty in understanding what Gong-sun Long was trying to demonstrate, for the debate seems to be taking place between the first speaker, who supports his assertion that a white horse is not a horse, and a second speaker who clearly thinks that the horses he encounters are still horses, whatever their colour. The

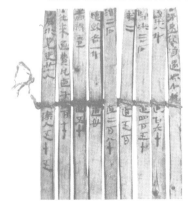

misunderstanding reached its height when one Western scholar proposed that the problem arose because an ancient Chinese book of Gong-sun Long's works, made up from bamboo strips laced together, had come untied and been reassembled in the wrong order. However, remembering that Chinese was written in ideographic characters, each of which conveyed a chunk of meaning, the traditional text makes perfect sense as a debate between one speaker who is looking at the physical world and another speaker who is dealing with how that world is to be represented in writing. Following the introductory statement, the debate runs as follows:

Gong-sun Long: I think that's allowable.

A.N. Other: How come?

Gong-sun Long: We use "horse" [the character 馬, *ma] to name the form, and we use "white" [the character* 白 *, bai] to name the colour; the naming of a form is not the naming of a colour. That's why I say, "a white horse is not a horse".*

A.N. Other: Suppose there is a white horse, then you cannot say that there is no horse. How can the fact that you cannot say that there is no horse allow you to say that the white horse is not a horse? The existence of a white horse implies that there is a horse – a white one. How can it not be a horse?

Gong-sun Long: If you are looking for a horse, chestnut and black horses both fill the bill. If you are looking for a white horse, chestnut and black horses don't fill the bill. Suppose a white horse were a horse. In this case what you are looking for is identical, and this being so a white horse is no different from a horse. Because what you are looking for is not different, as if chestnut and black horses are simultaneously allowed and not allowed, what follows? Possibility coexists with impossibility, a coexistence which is mutually exclusive. So the fact that a white horse is not a horse is proved in detail.

A.N. Other: If you argue that the fact that a horse has a colour means that it is not a horse, then since the world can't contain a horse which has no colour, is it correct to say that there are no horses in the world?

Gong-sun Long: Horses definitely have colours. Therefore there are white horses. Suppose that a horse had no colour, then you would simply have "horse" per se. How could that give you a white horse? Therefore the whiteness is not the horse. A white horse is "horse-ness" plus "white-ness". But if you propose "horse-ness" plus "white-horse-ness", I say that "white horse" is not "horse".

By this point in the debate it has become clear that what Gong-sun Long is talking about is the use of the ideographs 白 (*bai* – 'white') and 馬 (*ma* – 'horse') rather than any actual white horse. This conclusion is reinforced by another of his debates, this time about 'pointers' and 'things'. Although it has been suggested that the reference to a pointer corresponds to the ancient Greek philosophical concept of the 'form' of a thing, in the context of Gong-sun Long's debates it seems more direct to think in terms of the scope of meaning of a Chinese character, which obviously embraces 'things' in the real world, and the use of the character as a label which identifies – or points to –

that scope. A simple diagram will serve to show how this makes sense of Gong-sun Long's argument.

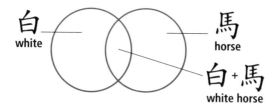

In the diagram, the character *bai* points to the area whose scope is 'white-ness', and the character *ma* points to the area whose scope is 'horse-ness'. For convenience, each area is visualised as a circle, and it is the area that is specific to the respective character. The area which accommodates things that have both horse-ness and white-ness is clearly not a circle, but has a lenticular shape. The scope of this area, which encompasses white horses, is clearly not the same as the 'horse-ness' circle, nor indeed of the 'white-ness' circle, so in terms of the way in which Chinese characters represent reality, Gong-sun Long is clearly correct in saying that 'white horse' (the lenticular shape) is not the same as 'horse' (the right-hand circle).

Some of Gong-sun Long's other debates – for example, the one which explores the statement that a stone cannot be both hard and white – can also be understood on a similar basis, but extended to consider cases where the areas pointed to by three characters overlap. So, one of the topics of interest to the School of Names was how to ensure correct use of Chinese characters to represent reality.

Significance of the School of Names

This account of the underlying reasoning in Gong-sun Long's debates is of more than purely linguistic interest. Remembering that Xün Kuang reserved the control of names (and therefore the use of language) to the ruler, it might at first sight seem unlikely that he would disagree with the philosophers of the School of Names, but he was particularly worried by the arguments of Hui Shi, who used his rhetorical skills to undermine common-sense notions of things – for example, in the paradox of the relative heights of mountains and swamps. For Xün, this was literally playing with words, depriving them of their proper meanings. In particular, he was afraid that the use by lawyers of School of Names arguments would bring about unjust results in litigation, defeating the purposes of the ruler in administering the state.

Nevertheless, the principles developed by the philosophers of the School of Names would form part of the platform from which the subsequent philosophy of Legalism would spring. As the various Warring States were amalgamated by conquest and treaty, the geographical areas to be controlled from the centre were becoming larger, and it became more important to develop administrative systems that depended on documents rather than word of mouth. The success of this development over the centuries is clear from the fact that it was eventually capable of supporting administration over such distances that the recipients of the centrally issued edicts were able to read and understand them, even though they spoke mutually incomprehensible dialects of Chinese. The key to this success was the nature of the Chinese characters, which, as we have seen, were pointers to areas of meaning. It was vital for the system to work that the respective area of meaning to which each character pointed was understood by all, and we can see in this the reasoning behind Xün Kuang's condemnation of the unilateral coining of names, which he felt would cause confusion in relation to regular names and so cause deception of the populace.

Despite Xün Kuang's opposition to the School of Names, Gong-sun Long's contribution to the subject was to explore exactly how the Chinese character writing system worked, and so to make it possible to use the characters to define information accurately. This would clearly aid in the framing of clear regulations, which in turn would promote good administration. The framing of regulations, however, was about to be wrested from the hands of the Confucian sages and seized by a new school – the so-called Legalists.

Chapter 10

Legalism

The Warring States

To follow the next step in our journey through Chinese philosophy, we need to look in a little more detail at the history of the Warring States.

If we were to study a map of China in 450 BCE, we would find the state of Qin located at the far western end of the area of Chinese culture. At the time, it was even felt by some of the other states forming the remains of the Zhou Dynasty that the people of Qin were not really Chinese at all. The people of the so-called 'Six Kingdoms' all followed Zhou culture, but the people of Qin, with their war-like attributes, including the use of horses in battle, were viewed as more like the external 'barbarians'. The feeling of 'inside' and 'outside' was emphasised by the evolution of long defensive walls not only between the states, but also as an outer bulwark against the nomadic tribes who inhabited the lands to the north and west.

As the Warring States period began, with increasing military activity facilitated by emerging iron-founding technology, the remains of the Zhou hegemony began to crumble when the state of Jin started to collapse in about 403 BCE. By 376 BCE it had split into the three distinct states of Zhao, Wei and Han.

The failure of traditional values

While the Warring States' rulers were struggling to maintain coherent administration in the face of increasing confusion in society, a new strand of thought was emerging. One key factor of traditional rule was the need to observe the Rites in maintaining a hierarchical structure in which all, from highest to lowest, were linked with ties of duties and obligations. This was always an idealistic concept, and, as society became more complex and the areas controlled by a state grew larger, the top and the bottom of the sociological pyramid became more and more estranged from each other. One writer expressed this phenomenon by observing that the Rites did not flow all the way down from the ruler to the populace at large, and that the punishments of the law did not extend right up to the ruling classes. This being the case, the mortar that in theory held the traditional state together had started to crumble.

This state of affairs led to the rise of a new generation of freelance advisers to the rulers of the states, whose approach was more pragmatic than traditional. They were not particularly concerned with the Rites, which had become discredited, but with the methods (法, fa) to control the populace.

Shang Yang

An early exponent of this new school of thought, conventionally called 'Legalists' from the use of the character *fa* in more recent times to refer to legal affairs, was Shang Yang (385–338 BCE), who was a  descendant of the royal house of Wei. The *Book of the Lord Shang* records his ideas, and in particular sets out his exposition of the case for a new standard for administration in the altered circumstances which had arisen as the Warring States period progressed. Shang Yang's approach was that the past was no longer a good guide for the present and future administration of a state. The Rites were past their prime, and pragmatic methods were needed to ensure order in the state.

As an indication of the significance of the Rectification of Names to Shang Yang, one of the chapters of the *Book of the Lord Shang* is entitled 'The Unification of Words'. This chapter deals with the approach that the sage ruler should adopt in administering his state:

Whenever a state is established, it is essential to maintain correct regulations and standards, to be

*careful about methods of government, to be attentive
to the duties required by the state, and to consolidate
the basis of affairs. If the regulations and standards
are maintained correctly the customary ways can
be adjusted and the people will follow the decision.
If the methods of government are clearly understood,
then the officials will be free from corruption. If
duties required by the state are consistent then the
people will respond so that they can be employed.
If the basic affairs are consolidated, then the people
will be happy in agriculture and enjoy battle.*

It is clear from this passage that Shang Yang
considered precision in formulating the policies of state
to be of paramount importance, and this clearly
included precision in the language used. In this he was
probably not far away from the position of Xün and the
School of Names, but in the last sentence quoted he
obviously takes a more belligerent foreign policy stance
than mainstream Confucianism. The reference to the
enjoyment of battle, taken together with the phrase
'the customary ways can be adjusted', is followed in
the same paragraph by the following passage:

*Therefore those who rule a state achieve
defensive strength by strengthening its military
forces through enrichment of the state; they
achieve offensive strength by encouraging the
populace to deal with enemies.*

Here we have the idea of a state which is run on highly
organised lines, and which is geared specifically to the

idea of warfare against neighbouring states. Such a state does not rely on the accumulated practices of legendary Sage Kings and their ideological successors, but adapts its policies to circumstances and sees strength in carefully formulated regulations and their practice.

Shang Yang had the opportunity to implement his radical ideas when the ruler of the state of Qin let it be known that he was looking for ideas to strengthen his state. Shang Yang went to Qin with his theories, and so impressed the Qin ruler that he was appointed Chancellor of Qin from 359 to 350 BCE, a role in which he applied his ideas to practical government.

One of Shang Yang's more important innovations was to break the hereditary principle which had been a long-established part of the traditional Zhou system, replacing it with a meritocracy in which individuals were to be rewarded in proportion to their service to the state. To manage the rewards Shang Yang set up a series of ranks, and an individual was accorded a rank that matched his degree of service. The privileges of rank increased as one ascended, and the higher ranks were awarded grants of land. The other side of the coin was a promulgated list of punishments, applicable to all irrespective of their rank. As with the social rankings, punishments were graded, from fines and compulsory service to the government, up through tattooing or mutilation to death.

Shang Yang also imposed strict controls at the level of the family or the community. He set up a system of 'responsibility groups', which consisted of five or ten people each, and in which each member was responsible for policing the behaviour of the group. If a group member committed a crime, the others were bound to report the matter to the authorities, on pain of punishment – not only for the offender but also for the group, if its members failed to report a crime committed by one of their number. In addition to this subdivision of society, individual households had to be registered for taxation purposes. However, each household was only allowed one able-bodied adult male. If there were more than one, all but the registered individual were required to set up new households in a developing area, so expanding the cultivated area of the state and establishing a new taxable unit from which the regime could extract taxes. The organisation of land was also centralised by the government, being allocated and laid out according to official regulations.

By such means the state of Qin developed a highly organised and motivated system of government, controlled from the centre; this was quite distinct from the traditional, 'feudal' way in which neighbouring states were ruled, which had influenced and been influenced by the Confucian cast of mind. This was perhaps another reason why the people of Qin continued to be viewed as 'not quite properly Chinese' by the other states of the time.

Han Fei

The thinking of Shang Yang formed a background against which followers of the *Xünzi* could develop a model of a state in which goodness was not part of the equations of government. Two of Xün's own pupils, Han Fei (280–233 BCE) and Li Si (280–208 BCE), were prominent respectively in the development of a Legalist model of government and its application in the state of Qin, which was eventually to conquer all the remaining Warring States and create a unified China from the political wreckage of the period.

According to Si-ma Qian, Han Fei came from the family of the Dukes of Han. He enjoyed the study of

Legalism[11]. It is intriguing that Si-ma Qian places Han Fei's biography together with the biography of Laozi, and claims that Han Fei's studies were grounded in the Yellow Emperor and Laozi. Si-ma Qian claims that Han Fei suffered from stuttering and could not speak properly, but that he was a skilled writer. Han Fei's book, known as the *Hanfeizi*, pulls together the known Legalist theories and sets out his views on how they should be understood if a state is to be well governed. The key to his philosophy is *fa* (法) – Regulations – which he saw as the ultimate basis of the state. In Chapter 38 of the *Hanfeizi*, he writes:

It is said that the quotation from Guan Zhong[12] 'a voice in a room fills the room, and a voice in a hall fills the hall' does not refer to mere entertainment or feasting, but must have some greater significance.

The most important matter for a leader of men is either Regulations or Statecraft. Regulations are organised in schedules and maintained in the official registry, so that they are manifest to the populace at large. Statecraft is concealed within the breast, and by the evaluation of countless details the ruler controls all the ministers in such a way that they are not aware of it. Therefore Regulations are eminently clear, but Statecraft does not reveal itself explicitly.

In this way an enlightened ruler proclaims Regulations so that within his borders there will be none among the populace who are not aware of them, not just 'those who fill a public hall' [that is, the small number who have visited the official registry]; he also uses Statecraft, in which case not even those closest to him will actually be aware of it – which is not even 'filling a private room' [that is, not even the close associates he would invite to a banquet]. So we can see that Guan Zhong's statement is not about Regulations and Statecraft.

In contrasting his own theory of Regulations and Statecraft to the quotation from Guan Zhong, which from his reference to it seems to have been used to derive guidelines for administration, Han Fei makes clear that Regulations need to be universally accepted in order that no one should be able to plead ignorance of them. As to Statecraft, this is, in Han Fei's view, a much more subjective matter, and it would seem that he felt that the ruler should play his cards very close to his chest in relation to his actual exercise of power. Knowledge of the Regulations should be adequate for everybody else.

What then was the nature of Han Fei's 'Regulations'? He used the character 法, which in modern Chinese signifies 'law', but in his time it did not have the same associations of jurisprudence. It was more a list of absolute rules set up by the ruler, with the intention that the rules themselves should provide the controls necessary for correct government of the country, and the ruler himself would not have to do anything further. If this sounds close to the Daoist concept that everything should be achieved by non-action, this is not surprising, as Han Fei devotes two chapters of his book to the lessons to be drawn from the *Dao-de Jing*, which he treats as a political text. So, the Regulations are themselves to provide a form of *dao* which all will naturally follow. The Daoists, however, would have distinguished themselves from the Legalists. In the *Zhuangzi*, it is argued that although the Legalists rely on punishments and rewards to manufacture a *dao* which will be followed by the populace without any effort on the part of the ruler, they do not understand the underlying Dao of the Daoists, and therefore are not in fact conforming to the fundamental nature of the universe.

What, then, underlies the Regulations by which the ministers of state are to conduct their business? To Han Fei the matter is very simple:

There are two tools, and two only, by which a
ruler guides and controls his ministers. These two

*tools are punishment and benefit.[13] What do I
mean by punishment and benefit? I call execution
'punishment', and rewards 'benefit'. Those who
are ministers are awed by capital punishment but
regard reward as profitable. Therefore if the ruler
practices punishment and benefit, then all his
ministers will be in awe of his majesty and
conform themselves to the advantage he offers.*

This 'stick and carrot' approach, in which failure by a
minister to conduct government according to the
Regulations is met with draconian punishments, while
the opposite is paid with great benefits, was the way in
which Han Fei and other Legalist philosophers and
administrators sought to maintain order in an age when,
as they saw it, life and politics had become too difficult
to rely upon the stately approach of the Confucians.

The third quality which Han Fei required in a ruler
was the ability to exercise power (勢, *shi*). By this
means the punishments and rewards could be enforced
on the populace at large, irrespective of their individual
virtue – which Han Fei believed was in any case a
rather rare phenomenon. He argued that within the
boundaries of a state, perhaps only ten people would
possess virtue, and so their attitudes need not be taken
into account when framing Regulations to control the
behaviour of the majority.

Another echo from earlier philosophies which crops
up in the *Hanfeizi* is the idea of the conforming of the
name to the reality. According to Han Fei the most
serious offence that any official could commit was
to fail to carry out a task that he, the official, had

undertaken. Han Fei justified this view on the basis that the task would in some way be defined. On the argument set out by Confucius as to the rectification of nomenclature, correctness of the definition would lead to successful completion of the task. Failure to complete the task, in Han Fei's view, meant that either the official's original specification of the task was faulty, or he had not achieved conformity between the specification and the desired outcome. In either case, the official was in breach of his duty.

Li Si

Han Fei remained in the state of Han, but his main work was as a philosopher who set out a coherent philosophy of pragmatic, self-sustaining government by which a state could be run, in contrast to his fellow student Li Si, who became an official under the Warring State of Qin. According to Si-ma Qian, Li Si did not consider himself the equal of Han Fei, but as things turned out it was Li Si who could be credited with the practical development of the Legalism of the state of Qin, so that it was fit to conquer the remaining Warring States and establish a single Chinese state.

Much of what we know about Li Si is contained in the *Shiji* of Si-ma Qian. Although not a native of the state of Qin, he became a high official in the state. Where Han Fei had consolidated Legalist thought into a coherent whole, Li Si took Legalist ideas and adopted them in government to ensure the absolute power of Qin. To Han Fei, with his speech impediment, written scholarship was his chosen means of expression.

However, while Li Si regarded farming and military prowess as the basis of the state, he regarded teachers and scholars as irrelevant and dispensable. Under his guidance, Qin became ever more powerful, and by means of military power and political manoeuvrings was eventually able to become the single Chinese state in 221 BCE. Along the way, in 233 BCE, Li Si betrayed Han Fei during the latter's embassy to Qin, possibly because of his jealousy of Han Fei's abilities and fear that Han Fei might supplant him (see below). All in all, Li Si was a ruthless man serving a ruthless state.

The State of Qin

In 334 BCE, after a period of quiescence in its western remoteness during which Shang Yang had been instituting his reformation of Qin's methods of government, the state of Chu began to expand to the south, and annexed Yue, which had not belonged to Zhou. Later, in 286 BCE, Chu conquered another of the southern states, Sung.

At about the time of the conquest of Sung, Han Fei and Li Si were growing up and would soon begin their studies under Xün Kuang. Han Fei would stay in his home state of Han for most of his life, but although Li Si gained a minor post in his home state of Chu, he became disillusioned with what he saw as the inadequacy of the king of Chu and the weakness of the alliance within which it was involved, and moved to the state of Qin.

References in the *Shiji* to the presence of Li Si in Qin begin with the reign of King Zheng, who at the age of thirteen succeeded King Zhuang Xiang in 246 BCE, by which time the state of Qin had already absorbed the states of Ba, Shu, and Han and had ambitions to take sole control of all the remaining Zhou states into the bargain. Si-ma Qian records that Li Si held a minor official post in Qin at this time. Immediately Qin began its campaign of attacks against the other states, defeating their armies and gaining territory. The military prowess of Qin was clearly demonstrated when in 241 BCE the five states of Han, Zhao, Chu and two states whose names are both transcribed as Wei mounted an attack on Qin, but their combined force was beaten by the Qin army. Force was not only used against the enemies of Qin, and when the Qin military failed, not only would the responsible general be executed, but all his men would also be executed. This is what happened in 239 BCE when King Zheng's younger brother led an unsuccessful rebellion. He was executed, his soldiers were rounded up, the officers committed suicide, and the inhabitants of the towns which had been involved in the rebellion were massacred.

We next hear of Li Si in 236 BCE, when he suggested to King Zheng that he should next take Han, as a warning to the other states. The king sent Li Si on a mission to undermine Han. The king of Han was alarmed, and plotted with Han Fei to weaken Qin.

In 233 BCE, Xuan Qi (a Qin general) attacked
Pingyang in the state of Zhao, killing General Yi She
and decapitating 100,000 Zhao troops. The next year
Qin again attacked Zhao, taking and destroying the
town of Yian and killing another general. Han Fei came
on an embassy to Qin, but King Zheng, following a plan
of Li Si, had him imprisoned and killed. Over the next
thirteen years, Qin's military and political might was
exercised in scheming and fighting to subdue all the
remaining Zhou states, and in 221 BCE the conquest of
the state of Qi completed the process. The influence of
Li Si in shaping the policies by which Qin secured this
success is undoubted, and becomes more apparent
from the historical record when we move on to consider
the consequences of Legalism through the rise and fall
of the unified Qin Empire.

Chapter 11

The Rise and Fall of the Empire of Qin

A Unified China

It's 221 BCE. The philosophy of Legalism has triumphed! The whole area that was once controlled by the House of Zhou is now under the control of a single administration, propelled to its position of supremacy by the Legalist philosophy of Shang Yang and Han Fei, implemented by Li Si, Chancellor of King Zheng of Qin, who now describes himself as Qin Shi Huang Di – the First of the August Emperors of Qin. Or was it as simple as that?

There is no doubt that the Qin Empire established total control of the Chinese territories, and was to secure that Imperial territory in a very short space of time indeed. The Legalist theory which had so successfully brought Qin Shi Huang Di to power was immediately extended from the government of the state of Qin to the administration of the whole Empire. The emperor was at the head of the administration, controlling a hierarchical system the next tier of which consisted of the Imperial chancellor and the Imperial counsellor. Below them was a complement of nine ministers of state, each with his own particular field of influence, including one whose responsibilities related to services and sacrifices to divine beings – not perhaps a particularly Legalist portfolio, but we shall return to that later. Below these top levels of the hierarchy, the officials at commandery and county level had their places. This structure worked through a counterflow of top-down edicts and bottom-up 'memorials' or petitions, which carried commands and requests respectively.

However perfect the framework, it could not of itself form a fully functioning government, and Qin Shi Huang Di provided the Regulations which were necessary to make it tick. To fund Imperial activities, a universal system of taxation was introduced, based as we have seen in the case of the Qin state on the household unit, and payable in kind[14] or in cash. Further demands could also be made on the populace in the form of compulsory labour service for the state, which was served in a variety of ways. Control of the populace at a local level was effected by an expansion of the Qin idea of 'responsibility units' to the whole Empire and at an

Imperial level by the extension of the institution of the ranks of honour. But the Regulations went into much more of the detail of everyday life than this, as can be read in a set of the Imperial Regulations dated 217 BCE and discovered in a cache of 1,100 inscribed bamboo slips found in a tomb near the city of Wuhan.

Evidence of the Legalism of the Qin Empire

The earliest Imperial edict to have survived so far actually dates from 221 BCE and not surprisingly, in view of its dating at the very beginning of Qin Shi Huang Di's reign, it is concerned with the basic nature of the Empire, setting out the way in which documents of state were to be formulated and specifying how memorials should be addressed to the emperor. This confirms that at the very start of the Imperial period in China, the aim of those administering the Empire was to create a well-organised bureaucracy. This was possible because there was, courtesy of the Confucian tradition, a well-established class of literate officials who would have been available to staff the bureaucratic offices of state. The nature of the edict also confirms the importance of precision to the Legalist mind, reflecting the emphasis that had been placed on the conforming of names to the realities which they defined.

The other notable aspect of the early Qin Imperial bureaucracy, as we can tell from the Wuhan slips, is that it covered pretty well everything to do with the conduct of life at all levels in society. Agricultural practice was specified, including stabling of animals and provision of granaries for crop storage. The format of the coinage was fixed. Financial practice for such matters as government inventories and accounting was laid out in detail. There were regulations for the employment of government officials, the conscription of workers for the state and the treatment of convicted criminals. Weights and measures were standardised, and government-approved standards were set for the purposes of checking and comparison, carrying inscriptions identifying their official origin. The gauge of carts was fixed, so that on rutted roads the wheels would be able to follow in the ruts left by the passage of earlier carts.

The detail of the regulations went down to a very fine level; the format of reports of damage to government property was specified in minute detail, and specifications were laid down on how objects marked with details of ownership were to be dealt with when discarded and the specific ownership changed. A range of punishments applicable for various crimes was prescribed, from the trivial up to torture and execution by the cruellest of methods, as were the procedures for the initiation and conduct of trials at various levels. Under the Qin Empire, standardisation of the written script was also a priority, to iron out differences which had accumulated between the characters used in the different states. The form adopted was distinctive in that it was specifically geared to the use of a writing brush, which had grown in use over the previous two or three centuries, rather than conforming to the patterns created by the sharp implements used for incised writing such as that found on oracle bones or bronze vessels.

This attention to the minutiae of government regulation ensured that so long as the regulations were observed and policed, the state could run smoothly with minimum intervention from the emperor. With secure control of the populace, the Qin Imperial government was able to embark on major civil engineering projects. Roads were constructed to ensure rapid passage for Imperial edicts to the farthest reaches of the Empire. Canal-building provided further transport routes and irrigation schemes. A huge mausoleum project was set in hand to provide a fitting last resting place for Qin Shi Huang Di when the time came. A major military construction project was also undertaken to link together existing lengths of defensive walls begun during the Warring States period to create a single wall protecting the northern and north-western flanks of the Qin territory. This concept of a boundary wall against the 'northern barbarians' was to be maintained more or less unchanged until a 'northern barbarian' race, the Manchus, seized control of China in the seventeenth century CE.

The appeal of traditional institutions

By means of these Regulations, set up under the auspices of Li Si, and with an energetic emperor in executive control at the top of the hierarchy, strong, centralised power was exerted across the Empire, and the superiority of Legalism would seem to have been established beyond any doubt. However, even under Qin

Shi Huang Di, concessions to earlier traditions seem to have been present. We have already seen that one of the ministers of state held a portfolio which was concerned with sacrifices. This is perhaps the first pointer, right at the dawn of Imperial government, to a phenomenon which was to recur throughout Chinese history, namely the tendency of an incoming regime, while overtly reviling its predecessor as an evil power that deserved to be overthrown, to absorb its predecessor's civil service and adopt many of the prevailing cultural traits. In the Qin Empire this tendency may also be observed in the many formal Imperial Progresses performed by Qin Shi Huang Di to the sacred mountains of China – sacred, that is, in terms of the earlier traditions – and his commissioning of stone inscriptions to record the event.

That is not to say that such acknowledgement of the alternative traditions was universal. In 213 BCE, Li Si began a large-scale destruction of earlier written material which became known as 'the burning of the books'. We now know that this was not a total destruction of all writings. Technical works dealing with practical matters like agriculture or medicine were not attacked, but anything that might substantiate allegations that the Qin ruler had abandoned the earlier traditions was condemned, and possessors of such material faced rigorous punishment. Later writers also alleged that 460 traditional scholars were put to death to prevent their views becoming known, but the historical accuracy of these allegations cannot be proved. Nevertheless, even on such a relatively un-melodramatic interpretation of the burning of the books, it is interesting to note that Qin Shi Huang Di, while not wishing to follow the traditional philosophy, was still sensitive about such allegations in the mouth of the populace, and indeed paid at least lip-service to the tradition in the Imperial Progresses.

The Death of Qin Shi Huang Di and the Collapse of the Qin Empire

Eventually, of course, Qin Shi Huang Di died, an event which took place during one of the Imperial Progresses. Li Si being chancellor, it is not altogether surprising, bearing in mind his track record, that the succession was not straightforward. Li and Zhao Gao, who was an official (possibly a eunuch, according to later writers, but this cannot be reliably confirmed), set their plan in motion. To give themselves time to get organised, they suppressed the news of the emperor's death, and placed a cart of dried fish next to his carriage in the procession so that the presence of the emperor's corpse would not be revealed as the body decayed. Zhao Gao seems to have been the instigator, and he moved to persuade the emperor's younger son, Ying Huhai, to accept the throne instead of Ying Fusu, the elder son, who was persuaded to commit suicide. Zhao Gao then saw to it that Meng Tian, the military official responsible for the establishment of Qin's defensive wall, was murdered. The remains of Qin Shi Huang Di were interred with due ceremony in his mausoleum, and Ying Huhai became the Second August Emperor, Er Shi Huang Di. A weak ruler, Er Shi Huang Di was effectively a tool of Zhao Gao, who seems to have attempted to control the Empire by increasingly severe punishments. Eventually this was counter-productive.

In 209 BCE a troop of soldiers detailed to report for duty on the defensive wall became so bogged down by torrential rains that they couldn't get there by the day specified in their orders, and they knew that if they were late reaching the wall they would be punished by execution. One of them, a man named Chen She, decided that they might as well raise a rebellion. The worst thing that could happen to them if the rebellion failed was death, he pointed out, but the rebellion, which might possibly succeed, was a better option than the certain death that awaited them if they simply continued to the wall. So they overpowered and killed the officers escorting them, and began the first recorded revolt against the Qin Empire. It did indeed fail, but in the days that followed, the collapse of the Empire under Zhao Gao and his puppet rulers

accelerated to such a degree that eventually, in 206 BCE, a man named Liu Bang, one of two contending outsiders, managed to conquer the Qin regime and supplant it with his own. He called it the Han Empire, using the name of one of the Warring States, with its appeal to the earlier Chinese traditions. So ended the fifteen-year Legalist experiment.

The Rise of Han

The Han Emperor, who had been known as Liu Bang but now took the official title of Gao Zu, set out to establish a new regime, which would be structured according to the precepts of Confucianism. Legalism had proved itself wanting as a civilised basis for government, and was to be consigned to history. Or was it?

There is no doubt that whatever its shortcomings in terms of oppressive controls and 'cruel and unusual' punishments, the Legalist underpinning of the administrative system of Qin had been a remarkably effective administrative machine. Regulations, however unpalatable, were clearly set out (as Xün Kuang himself would have required), and the duties and responsibilities of the bureaucracy were well defined. Defence of the state against external aggressors had been well secured, and trade and currency were regulated and sound. A network of roads and a system of mounted couriers had been established under the Qin to enable official edicts to be transmitted efficiently to all corners of the Empire, and the written script had been consolidated to ensure that all who received the edicts would be able to gain a clear understanding of their contents. Military technology was available to the incoming Han regime and so, as soon as Liu Bang's armies had successfully absorbed the remnants of the Qin troops, defence would be secured.

And yet, the backlash against the consequences of Legalist philosophy when used as an ideology for government by fallible human beings was profound. The imperial reign of Qin had been so short-lived that despite the burning of the books, the traditional ways attributed to Confucius and the Sage Kings were still well established in the minds of both rulers and people, and a programme was embarked upon to replace the Legalist basis of the state by a Confucian ethos in which the old qualities of human-heartedness, right behaviour and virtue, bound together in an all-embracing Dao, would reform the state for the good of ruler and people alike. Efforts were made to restore the Confucian Classics destroyed under the Qin Empire so that the state would be provided once more with its revered, if not sacred, texts, on which its renewed Confucianism would be built.

Education in the restored Confucian canon was seen as central to the evolution of an ethical bureaucracy, and the Han set out a scheme of things in which all would-be officials had to sit examinations based on the Confucian Classics. This central aspect of the Han bureaucracy was to continue, with limited interruptions, down to the twentieth century CE. The Rites once again became a vital part of Imperial and bureaucratic life and procedure. All would be well again. But . . .

You may have noticed in the preceding paragraph that the selection of officials, although Confucian in its basis, nevertheless depended on merit and not heredity. Families anxious for their sons to become officials had to ensure that they secured this through success in the Imperial examinations, and although corruption may have allowed some nepotism to succeed, the theory was of promotion by achievement in examinations – a remarkably Legalist principle! Similarly, the general techniques of administration that the Legalist-inspired Qin had applied were found by the Han to be remarkably effective and continued to be used, although the grosser inhumanities of the Qin were mitigated. From this point onward in Chinese history, there would continue to be a tension between the official Confucianism of the state and the influence of the civil service, which inevitably embodied systematic methods that were not unrelated to the Regulations and Statecraft of Legalism.

The influence of Confucian theory is clear from the continuation of the Office of History. Si-ma Qian, whose works have already been quoted in the present volume, was the head of the Office of History in the Han Empire and, with his son, compiled the *Shiji*, or *Records of the Grand Historian*, which was published in around 90 BCE. This was a massive undertaking, having as its aim the compilation of a written history spanning from the earliest legends of the Sage Kings, down to the founding of the Han Empire. It included histories and biographies drawn from extant documents as well as oral tradition, technical treatises on specialist topics such as hydraulic engineering, and many tabular presentations of information. Modern archaeologists have found that much of Si-ma Qian's writing is remarkably accurate, even where he probably had no actual source documents to work from. Si-ma Qian's office was also charged with maintaining an archive of all aspects of the Han Empire and, as we have seen earlier, this was consciously preserved to enable the Office of History in the next imperial regime to write the definitive history of the Han after the Mandate of Heaven had passed from the one to the other. This task was carried out faithfully across the millennia, and we have today a huge historical resource in the series of so-called Dynastic Histories that this thoroughly Confucian practice produced.

The continuity of the restored Confucianism, drawing its inspiration from the pre-Qin traditions of human-heartedness and right conduct, and administered by a loyal civil service, selected by merit, looked set to continue as the natural government style of China. The Chinese of Han, although they were aware of the continuing need to defend their territory from the northern barbarian tribes, were nevertheless very China-centric, and viewed their own civilisation as massively superior to all others, and it would have seemed to them impossible that any external influence could modify the conclusions that they had reached with the support of Confucianism.

Chapter 12

Buddhism in China

The Arrival of Buddhism

'Impossible' is a word that historians, as well as philosophers, should be wary of using. The Han had re-established Confucian philosophy as the guiding light of the emperor's rule, Legalism as a philosophy was discredited (however useful its ideas may have been to the administrators) and the anti-establishment nature of Daoism had been pushed aside, so the Confucian way ahead looked clear for the foreseeable future. Certainly the Confucians didn't contemplate that any barbarian thought could ever challenge the inherent superiority of the teaching of Confucius and his successors, but they hadn't reckoned on Buddhism.

Traditionally it was believed that Emperor Ming of the later Han Dynasty, who ruled from 58 to 75 CE, dreamed of the Buddha and sent an embassy to India to invite Buddhist monks to China. The story of the dream is undoubtedly legendary, but in fact the arrival of Buddhist monks in China can be dated as early as 65 CE, when they established a community in Pengcheng (in modern-day Jiangsu province) under the protection of a Han prince, Liu Ying, who was also a patron of Daoism. This arrival of alien ideas from an alien land was totally unexpected, but in the longer term it was to have considerable effects on the course of Chinese philosophy.

One advantage possessed by Buddhism as far as its eventual infiltration into Chinese thought was concerned was its 'otherness', which was not catered for by official Han Confucianism. In many aspects its strong philosophical core meant that it could be approached as a new development in philosophy. Another advantage arose because of the legends of the departure of Laozi to the western hills at the end of his life. This enabled Daoist-leaning thinkers such as Prince Liu Ying to assert that the Indian Buddhists had in fact learned their ideas of non-being from Laozi himself, so that Buddhism was authenticated as a 'Chinese' phenomenon and its scriptures (or *sutras*) as simply translations into Sanskrit of the *Dao-de Jing*.

Emergence of a Chinese Buddhism

Gradually some Chinese scholars began to explore Buddhism, and they started to translate the Buddhist *sutras* into Chinese. In so doing they applied the terminology of Daoism to many of the Buddhist concepts, further strengthening the case that Buddhism was in fact a teaching which was acceptable to a Chinese audience. Indeed, Buddhism in China developed a specifically

Chinese flavour as a result of these translations, the most significant of which was the development of the Chan school of Buddhism, more commonly known in the West by its Japanese name of Zen.

One of the core aspects of Buddhism, of whatever school, is the search for enlightenment, the spiritual achievement of separation of the soul from an otherwise unending cycle of life, death and rebirth. Traditionally, enlightenment was to be achieved by a diligent study of the teaching of Gautama Buddha, transmitted through the *sutras*, and it was understood that this achievement would be brought about by a gradual process of spiritual self-improvement leading ultimately

to the end-state known as *nirvana*. The Chan scholars and teachers, however, took a different line. Enlightenment would not occur, they believed, just as a result of diligent study, because the transition from one's ordinary appreciation of things to the enlightened state must always be a huge leap rather than a small, final step in a process. The Chan Buddhists therefore taught their pupils by posing questions which could not be logically answered – for example, the injunction to conceive of the sound of a single hand clapping – and, when the pupil had exhausted his mind in trying to find impossible answers, exposing him to a sudden shock such as a blow or unexpected noise, so that his consciousness would be hurled across the spiritual abyss that had previously separated him from enlightenment.

The Rise of Buddhism from Han to Sui

Buddhism would not immediately secure a huge following in China during the Han period, but in the less stable period from 222 CE, when the Han Dynasty fell, through the so-called Six Dynasties period, culminating in the Sui Dynasty (589–618 CE), there was a flourishing of Buddhism and the establishment of monasteries in which the development of Chinese Buddhism could be nurtured. This rise of the Buddhist monasteries enabled people who wanted to escape the chaos of political life to withdraw from secular Chinese society. There was also the fringe benefit of withdrawal from the taxation and labour obligations of Chinese citizenship. But the monasteries had one problem in their relationship to the Confucian-leaning state, in that one obligation of the citizen was to have sons who could continue to observe the Confucian Rites on behalf of the ancestors. To enter a state of monastic celibacy was to abandon this Confucian obligation, and this aspect of Buddhism in particular was to lead to antagonism between the state and the monasteries.

During the Six Dynasties period there was an explosion of Buddhist art in painting and sculpture that is known from archaeological excavations, and it is clear that in parts of China Buddhism developed a strong following, with the monasteries accumulating great power as adherents donated their wealth and lands to the Buddhist communities. This was to lead to political and economic struggles between the state and the Buddhist population, and these would come to a head under the Tang Dynasty (618–907 CE). This political situation meant that Buddhism tended to be considered as both politically and philosophically subversive of the state.

Buddhism under the Tang

The short-lived Sui Dynasty, which had reunited China following the Six Dynasties period, fell because of military over-extension in failed campaigns to conquer the Korean peninsula. The resultant economic hardship led to popular unrest and the eventual transfer of the Mandate of Heaven to a new regime, known as the Tang Dynasty. The Tang was to provide nearly three hundred years of united rule of China, and is known as a time of great literary and artistic creativity. One of its early achievements was the reintroduction of Confucian civil service examinations. The examination system ran alongside the hereditary practices surviving from the Six Dynasties period, but was extended during the Tang Dynasty so that it could increasingly provide the necessary officials versed in the Confucian canon who could run a Confucian administration.

One of the early problems of the Tang, however, was that of how to cope with a sizeable Buddhist population within the framework of a Confucian state. The first Tang emperor, Gao Zu, needed to balance the cost of the campaigns by which he had risen to power in 618 CE, and by 626 CE he had ordered a drastic purge of Buddhist clergy and action to confiscate the great wealth which the Buddhist monasteries had accumulated. In its proposals to reduce the number of temples, the order was also directed against Daoist establishments. Before the order could be put into effect, however, Gao Zu's sons successfully carried out a plot to take over the Imperial succession. One of the conspirators, Tai Zong, having subsequently killed his brothers and forced his father into retirement, then acted immediately to rescind the order.

Tai Zong, despite his apparently pro-Buddhist attitude, did not adopt Buddhism as a state orthodoxy. In 628 CE he commanded that a Confucian temple should be established in the Imperial University, and two years later he ordered the preparation of an official edition of the basic Confucian texts, together with new explanatory commentaries. On this basis, and despite the presence of a number of ministers whom we know to have been Buddhist in their personal lives, he maintained a basically Confucian state, although he did in the early

years of his reign honour Buddhist practices and among other things was instrumental in the establishment of Buddhist temples in memory of war dead. In the later part of his reign he was less prominently a Buddhist sympathiser, and indeed issued an edict to the effect that Daoist adepts were to have formal precedence over Buddhist clergy. There was also a move to have him declared to be a descendant of Laozi, which may have been part of an intention to gain a link to earlier messianic Daoist rebellions of the second century CE. But despite his attention to Buddhism and Daoism, Tai Zong in 637 CE commissioned an investigation into the history of Imperial Rites with a view to performing sacrifices on the sacred mountain, Mount Tai. In 641 CE he set out to do this, although the appearance of a comet, regarded as an inauspicious sign, caused the project to be abandoned.

The life and reign of Tai Zong, who died in 649 CE, shows clearly how the influences of Confucianism, Daoism and the newer Buddhism vied with each other in the Chinese consciousness, and the reference to both Buddhist and Daoist temples in the proscription of 626 CE indicates that there was an ongoing religious Daoism in China, in contrast to the philosophical Daoism of pre-Imperial times. Tai Zong's political skill was in maintaining a balance between the various strands, and implementing an administration which was at least nominally Confucian.

The reign of the Empress Wu

There was one point in the Tang Dynasty where Buddhism did achieve a very high profile. In 683 CE, Zhong Zong, the son of the previous emperor Gao Zong and his consort, Wu Zhao, was placed on the throne by his mother but deposed by her a mere two months later, when she took the Imperial throne as the only empress to have ruled China directly. She was conscious of the fact that Confucian theory made it impossible for a woman to become emperor, so she took advantage of a Buddhist *sutra* (the *Da Yun Jing*) which predicted that seven hundred years after the Buddha's death there would arise a pious woman who would rule an empire to which all other nations would submit. Wu Zhao argued that she was indeed the woman foretold by the *sutra*, and further that she was an incarnation of Maitreya, the future Buddha. In 690 CE the Empress Wu declared a new dynasty, the Zhou, of which she was the sole ruler until her death in 705 CE, after which the Tang Dynasty re-established itself under her son Zhong Zong. Although he personally was a devout Buddhist, Buddhism never again established such a high profile in official circles as it had done under his mother's reign.

Confucianism regained its earlier hold over the administration of the state, and there is evidence in the taxation system that there was a concerted attempt to model the administration on that of the Sage Kings of antiquity. An official manual of administration, the *Tang Liu Dian*, was drawn up between 722 and 738 CE. It was modelled on pre-Qin manuals of the Rites, and based its schedules of grain tax and commodity 'tribute' on the traditional accounts of the progress of Yu the Great in recovering the Chinese lands from the great flood of legend. This might be seen as window dressing, to 'prove' that the Tang emperors were good Confucians, but archaeological evidence makes it clear that the officials administering the tax system were straining to follow the manual to the letter. Inscribed clay tablets excavated from the Han Jia granary at

Loyang show that the procedures in the *Tang Liu Dian* were meticulously followed. More remarkable still, paper tax records, recycled to make grave clothes in the Central Asian deserts, have been deciphered and translated. They include records of goods collected, and a separate set of records of unpaid items. The latter includes entries such as 'The tax due from Li Yikang and Bao Zhuiwei is deficient', and even 'Today we got Li and Wang's deficiencies paid in'. Clearly the Chinese-appointed tax collectors were operating under difficulties. Perhaps the most remarkable find, however, is a bolt of linen fabric found in the grave of a minor official in Astana, now the capital of present-day Kazakhstan. It would have been a valuable item, part of his official salary, and it carried an official inscription giving its origin – 'Yun County, Guangdong district, from He Sijing, 1 roll of tax linen. Ninth year of Kaiyuan, eighth month [September 721 CE]. Special Officer Wang.' Yun County was in southern China, so the cloth would have been collected by officials, sent to the capital at Loyang and then transported to the central Asian city of Astana to pay the official's salary. The Confucian system was alive and well.

During the time of the Empress Wu, Buddhism had gained strong official encouragement, and there was a great deal of development in Chinese Buddhist thought. The empress herself sponsored translations of *sutras* from the Sanskrit, and appointed Buddhist monks to official positions in her court. This Buddhist tendency gradually faded from Chinese official circles after her death, until a rebellion led by An Lushan in 755 CE threw the Empire into a state of confusion from which it did not emerge until 763 CE. Nevertheless, through the political upheavals of the Tang Dynasty to this point, three distinct schools of Buddhism had established themselves in China, namely the Tian Tai school, the Fa Xiang school and the Hua Yan school. The Tian Tai school arose early, and was a developed Chinese form of Buddhism. It was eclipsed in the second half of the seventh century by the Fa Xiang school, which was a more emphatically Indian school, despite its representing a more primitive form of Buddhist thought than Tian Tai Buddhism. It was only after the death of the Empress Wu that Chinese-inspired Buddhism regained its sway, but it did so through the Hua Yan school. Each school based itself on a particular *sutra*, so they were in effect rivals within the Buddhist strand.

The role of An Lushan in the political fortunes of the Tang Dynasty is interesting in two ways. The official history of the Tang reports of him that he was of Turkic origin, showing that, rather like the first Qin emperor, he came from beyond the Chinese heartland, and also that his father was a shaman. This latter piece of information shows that the practice of shamanism, a form of occultism, survived into the Tang period, and was known about by the Chinese, whose own cultural spectrum, as we have seen, included religious Daoism. Although perhaps a minority interest among the so-called 'literati', occultism still had its adherents among the population, and both religious Daoism and Buddhism were to influence the next major development of Chinese philosophical thought.

After the An Lushan rebellion was over, the history of the Tang Dynasty became more fractured.

The Consolidation of Confucianism

Scholars were also regrouping after the ascendant phase of Buddhism. One notable document, written in 819 CE by the Confucian Han Yu (768–824 CE), was a memorial complaining to the Emperor Xian Zong about the ceremonial proposed to accompany the veneration of a purported relic of the Buddha. Han Yu began by categorising Buddhism as an imported barbarian phenomenon that drew nothing from prior Chinese traditions. He argued that Chinese decline during the Six Dynasties arose from the failure of the (vegetarian) Buddhists to use animals in ritual sacrifices, and sidestepped the Buddhist leanings of the early Tang emperors by blaming officials for not eliminating Buddhist and Daoist monks and nuns from China. Then he praised Xian Zong for deterring people from becoming monks and nuns and forbidding the construction of Buddhist and Daoist temples. He continued:

But now I hear that Your Majesty has commanded a multitude of Buddhist monks to welcome the Bone of the Buddha to Fengxiang, proposes to mount a viewing platform to watch as it comes into the enclosure and has commanded people from all the temples to observe the ceremonial. Although I am most stupid, I can only assume that Your Majesty is

not confused by the Buddha into performing this
veneration in order to seek prosperity from the gods.
It must just be because the people are happy at
harvest time, and to go along with the people's
feelings, that Your Majesty is making the capital
the site of a spectacle for high and low by means
of this charade.

Han Yu then warned Xian Zong that even so, the people would mistakenly believe that the emperor was a follower of Buddhism, and so would be led to follow Buddhism themselves, to their own disaster. Han Yu's recommendation to the emperor was to have nothing to do with the relic. Were Buddha alive, he argued, and had he come to China as a visiting ambassador, he would be treated to the normal courtesies but then escorted back to his own country. However, Buddha having died long ago, this 'foul rubbish of a rotted bone' should not be permitted to sully the Imperial court, without even so much as a shamanistic purification rite known from the legendary period.

Han Yu's objection to the veneration of Buddhist relics, and his reassertion of Confucian tradition, is typical of the resurgence of Confucian thought in the later part of the Tang Dynasty. As the regime disintegrated under a range of economic and military pressures, survival was perhaps more important than ideology, but the contribution of Han Yu and other Confucian scholars would be crucial in the general realignment of philosophical thought that would take place under the Sung (960–1279 CE).

Chapter 13

The Neo-Confucian Synthesis

Tang Confucianism

In addition to his *Memorial on the Buddha's Bone*, Han Yu also wrote essays on the topic of Confucian philosophy, one of which, *The Origin of the Dao*, made a reasoned distinction between Confucianism on the one hand and Buddhism and Daoism on the other, characterising the Dao of Buddhism and Daoism alike as internal and subjective, whereas the Dao of Confucianism was public and objective. His own traditionalist stance is clear from passages like the following:

> Now what do we mean when we talk of 'the teaching of the former Kings'? Their extension of love may be called Ren; their practice and approbation of Ren may be called Yi; conducting themselves on this basis may be called Dao; being self-sufficient without dependency on externals, may be called De. Their literature was the Odes, the Histories, the Book of Changes and the Spring and Autumn Annals; their laws were the Rites, Music, Punishments and Government administration; their populace comprised scholars and soldiers, farmers, artisans and tradesmen;

their relationships were between ruler and minister, father and son, teacher and pupil, guest and host, brothers, and husband and wife. Their clothing was of hemp and silk, their dwellings were palaces and houses; their food was cereals, rice, fruit, vegetables, fish and meat; what they practised as Dao was straightforward and enlightened, and their teaching was simple to achieve. ... What sort of Dao was this Dao? I say it is what I call Dao. It does not resemble what the Buddhists and Daoists call Dao. Yao took this Dao and transmitted it to Shun; Shun transmitted it to Tang; Tang transmitted it to the rulers of Zhou; the rulers of Zhou transmitted it to Confucius; Confucius transmitted it to Mencius. But at Mencius' death, it was not able to be transmitted further. Xünzi and Shang Yang confused it, their words on the subject were not accurate. Before the time of the Dukes of Zhou, the rulers were superior men, hence their actions succeeded; since that time, inferiors became ministers, hence mere words proliferated.

This reassertion of Confucian values is one aspect of the rethinking of the tradition that was going on in ninth-century Tang China. There were, however, other developments, which looked at the philosophical problems of the age in a broader light. One of the Tang philosophers in this area was a man named Li Ao. He was looking for a way in which Confucianism could accommodate the 'otherness' implicit in Buddhism and Daoism, and in one passage he says:

> How can a Sage be devoid of feeling? He is silently immovable; he arrives at his goal without travel, he is divine in his silence; he is enlightened without casting light. In acting, the Sage participates with Tian and Di; in his changes he accords with Yin and Yang. The Sage comprehends the feelings, but he is not subject to feelings.

Here Li Ao is discussing the subjective aspects of the sage's experience, and the whole of the essay from which the extract is taken is an exploration of how the sage must put feelings on one side in order to understand the natural order of things. This sense of detachment, as well as the concepts in the extract about, for example, arriving without travelling, show clearly that Li Ao was strongly influenced by Buddhist and Daoist values, and was trying to show how these subjective quantities could be expressed within a Confucian framework of understanding.

Han Yu's exposition of the fundamentals of Confucianism and Li Ao's exploration of how the kind of values which characterised Buddhism and Daoism made a key contribution to the development of philosophical thought that would take place in the Sung Dynasty, which came to power following the final collapse of the Tang regime and ruled substantially unchallenged from 960 to 1126 and then, after north China was seized by the Mongols, from 1127 to 1279 as the 'Southern Sung' Dynasty.

Transition to Neo-Confucianism

By the beginning of the Sung, Confucianism, Daoism and Buddhism all had their followings, and had set up permanent institutions by which their respective aims were to be fulfilled. Even the despised Legalism was implicit in what had now become the typical Confucian administration of the Chinese Empire. With all these strands pulling in different directions, attempts were made to promote a new form of unified philosophy that would be basically Confucian in nature, but would incorporate what we might nowadays call the 'metaphysical' aspects of Buddhism, Daoism and occultism.

The key item in this rebuilding of Confucianism was the concept of Dao, and its transmission from legendary times according to the account given by Han Yu and quoted above. In Chinese, the scholars who were involved were called the 'Dao Xue Jia' – literally, 'the experts in studies of the Dao'. This 'Dao Xue' is referred to in translation as neo-Confucianism, and its practitioners as neo-Confucians. Early in the Sung Dynasty the neo-Confucian movement comprised two main schools established respectively by two brothers from Henan province, Cheng Hao (1032–85) and Cheng Yi (1033–1108). The younger brother, Yi, founded the so-called School of Principles, and Hao established the School of Mind.

The central neo-Confucian figure in the Sung is Zhu Xi (1130–1200). He took over the development of the School of Principles, and brought it to a stage where it was the predominant school of neo-Confucian philosophy. Zhu Xi himself was a famous historian, a great commentator on the newly rehabilitated Confucian Classics, a renowned philosopher and a minor statesman. Cheng Yi's school takes its name from the character 理 (*li*, 'principle'), and Zhu Xi's idea was that all things have their metaphysical principle, which is then embodied in the physical things themselves. We may perhaps think of this *li* of a thing as a conceptual bundle of all the basic attributes of that thing. Although one might be tempted to draw a parallel with the 'forms' of the ancient Greek philosopher Plato, however, the Chinese turned out to be much more interested in the application of principles to human nature and society. So, for example, Zhu Xi used his concept of *li* to justify Mencius' claim that human nature is intrinsically good. He argued that the *li* of Man is pure, and so can be seen as the source of the basic virtues of humanity, including *ren*. However, the embodiment of this *li* in a particular individual is affected by the less-than-perfect nature of the individual and may need to be restored by education to recover its own purity. Self-cultivation also plays its part in the transformation of the human *li*, and may lead to an instant of sudden, Zen-like enlightenment.

The success of the neo-Confucian movement
The achievement of Zhu Xi and others in developing the neo-Confucian philosophy cannot be underestimated. The neo-Confucian synthesis gave the formal Confucianism of Han Yu the resilience it needed to provide an acceptable account of the human condition, with its need for metaphysical values, while retaining the authority of legend, antiquity, the Zhou rulers, Confucius and Mencius to support a state system of Confucian administration. Indeed, the neo-Confucian synthesis was to provide the central philosophy of successive Chinese administrations down to the twentieth century.

Chapter 14

From Tang to Qing

The Historical Perspective

In order to provide a context for what follows, we need once more to step aside from the purely philosophical development of China and look in more detail at the historical and religious background.

So far we have discussed a range of philosophies that all contributed significantly to the onward march of Chinese philosophy. The relative geographical isolation of China restricted the inward flow of new ideas, and only Buddhism, from relatively nearby India, had joined the main spectrum of Chinese thinking. Contact with Japan had come about in the ninth century CE when the Japanese monk Ennin had visited China, but the flow of ideas in that case was almost exclusively from China to Japan. There were also small communities of foreigners who practised Near-Eastern religions, mainly in the capital, Chang An, who are generally thought to have been involved in trade. Zoroastrians are documented as being in China as early as the sixth century CE, while in the early part of the Tang Dynasty Nestorian Christians and Manichaeans are found in the historical record – a Nestorian Christian memorial inscription dating from 781 still survives in modern-day Xi'an. There were also small numbers of Jews living in

China, and in the north-west of the country sizeable
Muslim populations developed thanks to the overland
trading route, the Silk Road.

None of these religious communities became
influential in China, however, so from the time of the
neo-Confucian developments of the Sung Dynasty the
indigenous philosophy of China went unchallenged
until the first concerted approach from the West,
marked by the arrival of the Roman Catholic Jesuit
mission to Beijing in 1600, in the final period of the Ming
Dynasty. This turned out to be the beginning of a long –
and for the Chinese, unhappy – relationship with the
emerging Western powers.

Christianity did not
spread widely in China,
either from the Nestorian
community of the Tang or
from the Jesuit mission,
whose influence was a
technical and scientific one,
based upon the Jesuits'
expertise in Western
natural philosophy. They
established an astronomical
observatory in Beijing

which survives to the present day, and also made their mathematical skills available to the Chinese court. From then on there would be tension in the court between the Confucian traditionalists and those who felt that the West had techniques to offer the Chinese. The main thrust of government and administration, however, continued on the neo-Confucian lines of the Sung philosophers, and China as a nation continued to regard itself as the whole of the civilised world, to whom all other countries should pay homage and, more practically, tribute. Even the emperors of the Qing Dynasty (1662–1912), although they were Manchus who had conquered the ethnic Han Dynasty of the Ming and rendered their Han subjects second-class citizens, nevertheless took over the Ming civil service more or less unchanged and themselves became the most Confucian of rulers, skilled in the literature and calligraphy of China.

Pressure from Europe

These *nouveaux Chinois* rulers, despite their own foreign origins, became traditionally Chinese even to the extent of maintaining the traditional Sino-centric view of China as Zhong Guo, 'the Middle Kingdom', and lording it over the unenlightened barbarian kingdoms. This policy led directly to the fierce conflict with Great Britain at the beginning of the nineteenth century. As the British expanded their empire in the eighteenth century, they began to trade with China, and by 1793 were looking to balance the trade in Chinese exports to Britain by some comparable exports of British goods to China. Pressure for this advance was fuelled by the products of the Industrial Revolution in Britain, and supported by the British government of the day.

The year 1793 marked the eightieth birthday celebrations of Qian Long, the Qing emperor, and Lord Macartney was sent as an ambassador to Beijing to convey Britain's congratulations on the occasion. The British demands presented by Macartney were an exchange of ambassadors between the two countries, the admission of British ships to more ports on the Chinese coast, the fixing of trade tariffs and the making available to the British of an island base similar to the Portuguese base at Macao. However, the British had failed to understand what the attitude of a Chinese emperor would be. They assumed that Britain, as a powerful modern state, could negotiate with China as an equal party; Qian Long, on the other hand, saw Britain as just another tributary state paying homage to the Middle Kingdom. The only concession Lord Macartney secured from

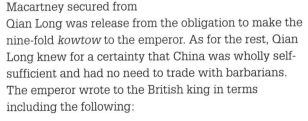

Qian Long was release from the obligation to make the nine-fold *kowtow* to the emperor. As for the rest, Qian Long knew for a certainty that China was wholly self-sufficient and had no need to trade with barbarians. The emperor wrote to the British king in terms including the following:

You will not be able to complain that I had not clearly forewarned you [about the restriction of British trade to the port of Canton only]. Let us therefore live in peace and friendship and do not make light of my words.

Despite the implied snub, the British decided to reply, and in 1795 wrote a letter to the emperor, accompanied by gifts. The emperor replied in kind, but it was made quite clear in his reply that, rather than gifts, 'tribute had been sent by the King of England to the "Son of Heaven"'.

Such mismatches between the attitudes of the British and the Chinese were to lead to ever-increasing friction between the two empires, complicated by the fact that at this time the 'British' forces in the area were actually the armies of the British East India Company, a private organisation.

The Opium Wars and the Tai Ping rebellion

Two major conflicts then arose in the nineteenth century, known as the First and Second Opium Wars, in which British and other European trading and commercial interests were ranged against the Chinese armies and navy and the Chinese suffered significant military defeats.

The First Opium War (1841–42) was settled by the Treaty of Nanking, according to which the Chinese were required to pay to Britain an indemnity of 21 million silver dollars, to open five Chinese ports to

British trade and to cede Hong Kong to the British. In addition to these impositions on China, there was considerable economic and trading disruption in South China. Some trade had been carried out in the Shanghai area, but after the war ended, much of this was transferred back to Canton, and poverty and hardship rose sharply around Shanghai. This led to the eruption of perhaps one of the most unexpected Chinese revolts against the Imperial government.

During the Qing Dynasty there had been a pattern of Buddhist- and Daoist-inspired rebellions against the regime, with groups such as the White Lotus sect and the Society of Heaven and Earth carrying out sporadic revolts and getting crushed each time by the Imperial armies. Now, however, a new indigenous rising took place, inspired not by the traditional anti-establishment movements but by Christianity. Its leader, Hong Xiuchuan, came from the Hakka people of south China, and was born in 1814 in a village about thirty miles inland from Canton. It is worth considering this 'Tai Ping' rebellion, since not only is it one of the great 'what if?'s of more recent Chinese Imperial history, having nearly overthrown the Qing Dynasty, but it also sheds light on the relationships between the Confucian system and the increasing exposure of the Chinese Empire to Western culture.

Hong was educated in the Confucian classics, and entered the civil service examinations several times, but without success. On one occasion when he was in

Canton for the examinations, a Chinese convert of a Protestant missionary, Robert Morrison, handed to Hong a book about Christianity. Hong pocketed the book, but the historical record does not reveal whether or to what extent he read it. On the basis of what happened later, however, it is probable that he did at least glance at its contents before filing it away with other miscellaneous papers when he got home. It then seems that in the depression of yet another examination failure, Hong fell ill for a period of some weeks, during which time he claimed that he had had visions of being in a vast palace where an old man sat enthroned; the old man handed Hong a sword and commanded him to cast out demons to protect his brothers and sisters. Also in the vision was a middle-aged man whom Hong had to address as 'Elder Brother', and who accompanied him on his quest. Hallucination merged at that point into delirium, and Hong sprang from his bed, striking out at all around him.

Hong appeared to be greatly changed by these events, and he set off to open a school in a nearby village and become a teacher. Six years later, in 1843, a relative visited him and unearthed the book from the pile of documents in which it had languished since Hong's vision. The relative saw what the book was, and teased Hong about owning such a work. Then, apparently for the first time, Hong read the book in detail, and in astonishment saw how the Christian doctrine in the book explained his vision, the old man representing the Christian God and the 'Elder Brother' being Jesus. The demons Hong had been commanded to defeat were the idols which the book said should be thrown down.

So inspired, Hong immediately baptised himself and his relative, founded a 'Society of God' and set out to fulfil the command from the vision. This immediately set him in opposition to his Confucian contemporaries, since in Hong's view, the idols which were to be destroyed included family ancestral tablets. To a Confucian, this action would have been the antithesis of everything for which Confucianism stood, and he rapidly lost pupils from the school he had set up. So Hong was forced to take his new beliefs elsewhere, where he almost immediately got into further trouble when he desecrated a Daoist shrine, thus offending a specifically religious sector of society. He then returned to his native village, while a Hakka colleague, Feng Yünshan, continued to a place called Thistle Mountain, where he set up as a teacher to the sons of local farmers and continued to recruit members to the Society of God.

Hong, meanwhile, was busy writing what would become the scriptures of his movement, and he recognized that the doctrine of the role of God as an omnipotent father whom all should worship was in direct opposition to the Confucian tradition that only the emperor was able to conduct the Rites to Heaven and Earth. Hong explicitly posed the question: 'God the Heavenly father is available to all; how can any prince monopolise the right to worship?' Having come to this point in his thinking, Hong tried to seek more information from the publishers of the book which had started all this off, and in 1847 he contacted an American evangelist in Canton, the Reverend Issachar Roberts. Roberts doubted Hong's understanding of Christianity, and was also unsure of his sincerity, and when Hong asked for baptism – in case his self-administered rite had not been effective – Roberts refused. Rebuffed, Hong returned home, but then heard of Feng's success at Thistle Mountain and joined him and the three thousand supporters he had gathered.

From that point the Society of God grew rapidly and became unpopular among traditionalists because of its attacks on shrines and temples in the neighbourhood of Thistle Mountain. A turning point in the Society's fortunes came when one of the wealthier landowners in the area sent men to seize Feng and present him to the local magistrate on charges of disturbing the public with false teachings. Despite Hong's efforts to have Feng released under the provisions of a new edict on religious toleration which the French had extracted from the emperor, Feng remained in prison. With both Feng and Hong absent the leadership vacuum was filled by two charcoal-burners who claimed to be possessed by God and Jesus, and were accorded positions by the Society above that of Feng.

This changed the dynamic of the Society at the same time as it continued to expand at a pace that inevitably widened its sociological membership. Prosperous landlords joined, one of whom, Wei Changhui, took the opportunity to fortify his farm as a base from which to raid his rivals' fields. This fatefully linked religious enthusiasm and armed force in the Society. Conditions in Guangdong province were such at the time that the Society of God attracted little attention from the authorities, who had more pressing problems of control to deal with, but in 1850 matters came to a head. Militia were dispatched by the authorities to arrest a known outlaw, but the troops involved took it upon themselves to rob the local inhabitants as well. However, the intended victims were not just a group of simple charcoal-burners, but keen members of Hong's society, and they routed the militia. One of the Society's more prosperous members was also travelling through the district en route to Thistle Mountain, and when he came across one of the defeated militia's camps, he sought revenge on behalf of the Society by detaining the leader's concubine. This act led directly to a declaration of war, made at the farm of Wei Changhui.

By 1851, the Society had declared a new dynasty, called the Tai Ping Tian Guo (太平天國) or 'Heavenly Kingdom of Great Peace' at a village called Yong-an (literally, 'eternal peace') in Guangxi province. The choice of this village, with its auspicious name, was probably not accidental, and the term Tai Ping Tian Guo itself was intended to resonate at a theological level. Hong himself wrote a commentary on the Gospel of Matthew including the passage:

Tian Guo refers to what is above in the sky and what is below on earth, for both are the Divine Father's Kingdom of Heaven. Do not be deceived

into thinking that it refers only to a kingdom in
the sky. So when the Heavenly Elder Brother
says 'the Kingdom of Heaven is at hand' he is
predicting the establishment of Tian Guo today
by the Heavenly Father and the Heavenly Elder
Brother.

The term 'Tai Ping' was less rigorously applied. The
Chinese term implies a degree of uniformity or equality,
and in theory this was the official view among Hong's
followers, but in practice the Tai Ping Tian Guo was to
have an aristocracy, albeit one in which the term
'emperor' was reserved for God, with Hong ranked as
Heavenly Prince, or Lord, and sundry other princes and
guardians. This aristocracy also maintained concubines
with official titles, whereas the rank-and-file followers
were expected to be celibate. Then, as the dynasty
consolidated itself, the aristocracy adopted court dress
in the style of the Ming Dynasty, and imposed
draconian punishments for any rank-and-file member
who was felt to have insulted the dignity of the
members of the hierarchy.

The Imperial government could clearly not tolerate
such actions, and sent a large army to Guangxi
province to eliminate the threat. They surrounded
Yong-an, but the Tai Ping broke the siege and marched
towards the provincial capital, Guilin. This was the
start of a campaign in which the Tai Ping armies took
control of a large area of south China. Two events
frustrated their ambitions, however. Firstly, having
captured the city of Wuzhang on the Yangtze River
from the Imperial forces, they decided to extend their

campaign further down the Yangtze to secure the wealth of Nanjing, rather than moving upstream into Sichuan, which they could have used as a springboard to attack the Imperial capital at Beijing. The decision was probably inspired by the fact that Nanjing had been the base of the founder of the Ming Dynasty when he defeated the Mongol Yuan Empire, but the state of the Imperial army after repeated defeats by the Tai Ping rebels was such that an attack from Sichuan would almost certainly have succeeded. The second event frustrating Tai Ping ambitions was the outbreak in 1857 of the Second Opium War, which unified China against the Western Powers.

The final act of the Tai Ping rebellion happened after the conclusion of the Second Opium War in 1858, and was accelerated by in-fighting among the aristocratic survivors of the Tai Ping Tian Guo, leading to final defeat in 1864. Confucianism secured this limited internal triumph and the rule of the emperor once again controlled the bulk of Chinese territory, but the Empire had suffered not only the shock of a nearly successful internal challenge based on an alien ideology, but also a devastating external defeat by the Western powers. The latter was made worse by the loss of face involved in the Treaty of Tientsin, by which the Second Opium War was settled, known by the Chinese as one of the 'unequal treaties'.

The support attracted by the Tai Ping rebellion, and the speed with which it spread, show how easily a charismatic leadership could serve to rouse a disaffected population against the Imperial authorities, despite the fact that it espoused an alien ideology.

Chapter 15

The End of the Confucian Empire

Attempts at Reform

The immediate aftermath of the Second Opium War saw the birth of a debate between traditionalists and reformers in the Qing Imperial court. The traditionalists continued to be of the opinion that China, the Middle Kingdom, was self-sufficient and simply needed to be better at what it did. The reformers felt that China's defeat was due to its failure to match the victorious Western powers, particularly in terms of military hardware, and that it was vital to study and apply Western science and technology to redress the balance.

A key player in this period was Li Hongzhang, the provincial governor of Jiangsu and Zhejiang in south-eastern China. Li led government forces in the final showdown against the Tai Ping, but in 1864 he sent a memorial to Prince Kong, one of the modernisers at court. His memorial emphasises that the traditional education system for the civil service is 'divorced from reality', with officials more concerned with the classical texts and calligraphy than with practical affairs. He also proposed that the mandarinate should have a new division of technically qualified officers who could understand and apply the methods of the West. A severe problem for the reformers was the fact that for the remainder of the nineteenth century the debate on the need for modernisation took place against a bitter and often violent background of disputes between various claimants to the Imperial throne, and their consorts and factions. Such attempts as there were to emulate Western technology were not always successful, and from 1875 to 1908 the Imperial power was effectively exerted by the Empress Dowager Yehonala, whose main concern seems to have been the establishment and

retention of her own power by any available means, supported by palace factions, during the reign of the puppet Emperor Guang Xu, who had been only three years old when he ascended to the Imperial throne.

In the early 1890s war broke out in northern China between China and Japan, and ultimately Japan inflicted a humiliating defeat on the Chinese forces. The Treaty of Shimonoseki, which ended the hostilities, imposed great territorial penalties on China.

Li Hongzhang summoned a Cantonese man called Kang Yuwei to court. Kang had initially failed the Imperial examinations and set up his own Confucian school, but eventually passed and began to publish his own ideas about government based on the ideas he had developed in his teaching, in which he sought to graft Western history and philosophy on to a basis of Confucianism. He held that Confucius had in his own day been an innovator, grafting his ideas on to the ancient traditions about the Sage Kings, and argued that it was justified to do this all over again in the face of the challenge from the West. He wrote a book entitled *Utopia*, in which he suggested that the governments of national states would merge into a world government and society would in essence be communal.

The 'Hundred Days' of reforming legislation

On Kang's arrival in Beijing in 1898, the idea of reform was put to the Guang Xu Emperor, but his main supporter at court, the elderly Prince Kong, died. Guang Xu was then faced with the choice of submitting once again to the political power of the anti-reform Empress Dowager and her faction, or relying upon popular support to introduce reform. He chose the latter course, and for a time a stream of reforms, clearly inspired by Kang Yuwei, flowed from the court, aimed at education, industry, banking, the press, the examination system and the armed forces. The Empress Dowager was incensed, and plotted the removal of the Emperor and reversal of the reform programme. After 103 days, the emperor submitted once more to the Regency of the

Empress Dowager, the reforms were stopped and six of the leading reformers were executed. The Empress Dowager's version of Confucian rule had triumphed, and the Emperor spent the rest of his days in close confinement.

The Boxer Rebellion

After these events it was once again the machinations of the Empress Dowager which led both directly and indirectly to the events of 1900 known as the Boxer Rebellion. From 1895 Shandong province in north-east China suffered increasing incursions of European and Japanese interests, and naturally enough the local Chinese began to protest. One focus of discontent was the White Lotus sect. This sect, which took its name from a fourteenth-century Buddhist-inspired group which had opposed the alien Yuan Dynasty, arose in the early years of the Qing to oppose its alien Manchu rulers. The ambition of the sect was to rebel against local oppression and extend this to a more general rebellion against the dynasty itself. By the end of the nineteenth century the White Lotus had been inactive for decades, but it emerged in 1896 with a new enemy, namely the Western powers, and its stance shifted to support for the dynasty against alien intruders, especially Christian missionaries, and Chinese Christian converts. One characteristic of the White Lotus was its stress on armed and unarmed combat, and its adherents soon became known as the Boxers. They claimed supernatural powers against blade and shot, and when the Empress Dowager heard of them they were invited to the capital, where they would

soon become involved in the notorious siege of the Legation Quarter in Beijing in 1900 – in this they were joined by fanatical Muslim soldiers from Kansu, who shared with the White Lotus sect a hatred of Christianity. The siege has become universally known as the Boxer Rebellion.

The conflict began with the murder of a Japanese diplomat and the German minister Baron von Ketteler, and on 20 June 1900, the Boxers attacked the Legation Quarter. Three days later an Imperial edict was issued declaring a state of war and instructing the governors of China's provinces to send troops. The major governors refused to comply, and instead offered their services to the foreign powers. A military response to the Boxers was set in train, and a relief column, which arrived at Beijing in mid-August, found the besieged foreigners still holding out and crushed the rebellion. The Empress Dowager fled from the Forbidden City to Xi'an, taking Guang Xu with her and pausing only to order her eunuchs to throw the Emperor's favourite concubine down a well. The Western powers then proceeded to sack Beijing.

The West, and in particular the German field-marshal Count Waldersee, wanted to pursue the court to Xi'an to settle matters once and for all, but the diplomacy of Li Hongzhang prevailed, and the Empress Dowager's regime survived, although on the Chinese side this was effected only after the execution or enforced suicide of a number of her senior advisers. The regime did not emerge unscathed, however, as the Western powers imposed an indemnity payment of 450 million dollars, an enormous sum which was raised from the Chinese customs dues and salt monopoly. There were other concessions extracted from China, one of which was the suspension of the civil service examinations, an action directed specifically against the literate middle classes who were felt by the West to have encouraged the Empress Dowager in her actions.

And so ended the grip of Confucianism on the Chinese administration, for the examinations would never be reinstated.

The Final Collapse of the Qing Dynasty

Beaten by the Western powers, suffering under another 'unequal treaty', and with its Confucian examination system abolished, the Qing Dynasty was an administrative vacuum waiting to be filled – and there would be no shortage of volunteers to fill the gap. The watchwords were 'science' and 'democracy', and the philosophical stance of the reformers would be above all pragmatic, in reaction to the elegant theory and ritual formality of Imperial Confucianism. One powerful opponent of the regime was a reformer, Liang Qichao, who had escaped to Japan from death at the hands of the Chinese court in 1898 and was writing as a journalist. Through his writing, he gave other Chinese reformers a vital tool in their fight for modernisation. Since the middle of the nineteenth century, Japanese authors had been coining new words for Western concepts using Kanji, the Chinese characters which are used in the Japanese writing system. Liang took over these neologisms unchanged and used them in his journalism, thus enabling Chinese thinkers to come to grips with the new Western-based knowledge.

Another individual who was to be instrumental in the emergence of China from its Imperial past was Sun Yat Sen, who in fact came from a family with links to the Tai Ping. Sun left China for Hawaii when he was eight years old and there became a Christian, studied medicine in Hong Kong and practised as a doctor in Macao. His background being so non-Chinese, he had difficulty in getting his ideas on modernisation accepted, despite having submitted a memorial to Li Hongzhang on the need for the civil service to include technical specialists. After this, Sun set up a republican secret society among sympathisers in Hawaii. After the Treaty of Shimonoseki was signed and its terms reducing the Chinese army were implemented, Sun recruited ex-soldiers to mount an armed attack on the residence of the governor of Canton. It failed, and Sun became a wanted man. When in exile in London, he was kidnapped by Chinese government agents but managed to get a message to his old Hong Kong medical professor, and when the news of his kidnapping was reported in the British press, the Chinese Legation in London was forced to release him. This event secured for Sun a great reputation among Chinese opponents of the Imperial regime.

Opposition to Qing rule was on the increase from sources such as these, and in 1905 a party of five senior Chinese officials set off on a fact-finding mission to Europe, to discover as much as they could about the workings of constitutional government. On their return, they reported that the only way of preventing a revolution was to introduce a constitution. The court, however, took an extremely narrow view of what a constitution might entail, and in the event the element of change was very small. According to the draft  constitution that was published by the court in 1908, the Emperor retained absolute power, had total control over law, justice and the army and could call or dissolve a national assembly at will. Freedom of speech, assembly and property were available 'within the law' but could be instantly withdrawn by Imperial order at any time. This constitution was never to be adopted. Later in the same year, the Emperor Guang Xu died, and the Empress Dowager manoeuvred the infant Pu Yi, the Emperor's nephew, into the succession, with Pu Yi's father as regent. Guang Xu's widow would inherit the title 'Empress Dowager', but Yehonala, now Grand Dowager, would be in charge. Aged seventy-three, in apparently good health, she had navigated yet another twist in the Qing Dynasty's history, and the next morning was involved in discussions of state – but as she arrived at the lunch table she collapsed, and that afternoon she died. On her death-bed she issued a decree that all important decisions should be taken by the regent on the instructions of the new Empress Dowager, who was her niece.

The final act

The end of the dynasty was now imminent. There were problems between the court and the governor of the Metropolitan Province, in which Beijing was located; the court, although wishing to extend its power over the provinces, was saddled with the constitutional programme of the Empress Dowager, which required the setting up of provincial assemblies whose membership, together with that of the consultative college, resulted in stalemate between reformers and court representatives; and finally, it transpired that when cabinet government was to be introduced in 1913, ten out of the thirteen cabinet ministers were Manchus, of whom six were Imperial princes.

In 1911 the final act began. The police in Hangou, near Wuzhang on the Yangtze River, were sent to investigate an explosion in the Russian Concession, and they found that the building was being used as an arsenal. As well as armaments, they also found a list of members of a revolutionary plot, many of whom were disaffected officers of the Wuzhang garrison of the Imperial army. On hearing that the list had come into the hands of the police, the conspirators rose in revolt on the night of 10 October. They secured Wuzhang, then crossed the river to occupy Hanyang and Hangou and approached the Hubei Provincial Assembly, who declared a Military Government of Hubei. This rebellion spread to the majority of Chinese provinces, and on Christmas Day, 1911, Sun Yat Sen landed in Shanghai, to be elected temporary president of a new Chinese Republic. He took up office on 1 January, 1912. On 12 February, 1912, the Empress Dowager issued an edict on behalf of the emperor, in which he yielded his authority 'to the country as a whole' on the grounds that the Will of Heaven made the decision inevitable. So, at the last, Confucian rule in China was ended on expressly Confucian grounds.

The reformers' stated ambition was to establish a stable Chinese Republic that would be able to take its rightful place among the other modern nations of the world, but in practice the political scene in China from 1911 was far from stable. Factional struggles between various powerful leaders led to a situation in which local warlords vied for position, and levels of corruption were certainly no less than they had been under the Empire. Much of the rural population suffered under economic hardship imposed by extortionate landlords to whom they were almost permanently in debt, and pressure built up towards another rebellion against the state, fuelled by a philosophy from outside China itself.

Chapter 16

Philosophy after the Empire

Western Philosophy in China

It was not until the very late nineteenth century that Chinese scholars began to study Western philosophers. For example, Yen Fu, who had been sent to England to study naval science, read the works of many English philosophers, including Huxley, Smith and Mill, and translated them into Chinese. After the Sino–Japanese war (1894–95) his translations were widely read in China by those who believed the country could be transformed by Western thought. He also translated Montesquieu's *Esprit des Lois*, and Wang Guowei, a historian of philosophy, translated Schopenhauer and Kant.

In the early twentieth century, Beijing University taught philosophy, and in 1915 a proposal emerged to open a Department of Western Philosophy, but the death of the Professor brought this to a premature end.

Of the Western philosophy of the eighteenth and nineteenth centuries, only Logic became an integral part of Chinese philosophical thought, through a seventeenth-century translation (by Li Zhizao in collaboration with Jesuits in Beijing) of a medieval work on Aristotelian logic, which appealed to the Chinese because of superficial resonances with the essays of Gong-sun Long.

Chinese in the West

The early years of the twentieth century saw a great interest in Western philosophical and political thought among the growing number of Chinese who were working and studying in Europe. They were to have two key impacts on the intellectual life of China. First, they became more familiar with Western ideas, particularly those of Marx and Engels. Secondly, and more immediately, there were Chinese in France at the time of the making of the Treaty of Versailles in 1919 that defined the settlement after the First World War. After initial neutrality, the Chinese had entered the war after attacks by Japan, and it was hoped that the Versailles treaty would return foreign-held Chinese territory that Japan had seized. In the event, Japan got the right to dispose of the German-held area of Shandong, and the Chinese delegates to the Versailles conference refused to sign. This news, telegraphed to Beijing, aroused great anger, and on 4 May the students of Beijing University demonstrated against the Treaty. They identified one of the greatest obstacles to Chinese progress as the archaic written form, known to the West as 'Classical Chinese', which was largely unchanged from the Zhou Dynasty, and did not directly reflect the spoken language. An unsuccessful attempt had been made in 1907 to represent the vernacular in written Chinese, and one of the students' key demands was for the replacement of Classical Chinese by a written form, known as 'baihua', based on speech, which could be understood more easily by non-scholars. This time, reform succeeded, and so another link to the classical Confucian past was broken.

The Birth of Communism in China

The arrival of Marxism in China was to have a major influence on Chinese affairs for the remainder of the twentieth century and beyond, and the May Fourth Movement provided a fertile bed for ideas of revolution based on popular discontent. By 1919 Marxist study groups existed in many Chinese cities. Gregor Voitinsky, a member of the Soviet Comintern, set up the first Communist Party branch in Shanghai in 1921. Marxism-Leninism rapidly became the main ideology of the disaffected population, and following the collapse of Confucianism at the end of the Empire and the repressive actions of the warlords of the Republican era, it became the dominant philosophy. The history of Communism in China under Mao Zedong is well known, and by 1949 the Communists had assumed power in China.

The attack on tradition

One of the key targets of the Chinese Communist Party (CCP) was that of traditional Chinese culture. For example, Classical Chinese documents had been a specialist field since 1919, but in the 1950s the Minister of Culture, Guo Moruo, introduced a simplification of the Chinese script, hoping to make Classical literature even more remote than the baihua reform had done. The effect was illustrated when the author visited Xi Bei University in Xi'an in the 1980s and started to read an eleventh-century copy of the *Shiji* on display in the library. The librarian expressed surprise, as he himself was unable to read it.

Under Mao, study of the Classics was discouraged and mass literature was Marxist-Leninist polemic seen through the lens of the CCP. Rigid Party control was established over the whole country. For forty years traditional philosophy and history were discarded, except for examples of proletarian courage and insight to support the Marxist-Leninist-Maoist line. Even technology and industry had to comply, the slogan 'better Red than expert' underpinning such disasters as Mao's 'Great Leap Forward' and 'Great Revolution of Proletarian Culture' in the 1970s and '80s. The only indigenous Chinese philosophy reflected in the period of Mao's leadership of the CCP was Legalism. Rules abounded, punishments could be draconian, and the neighbourhood groups whose members were expected to inform on each other were an echo of the fourth-century BCE policies of Shang Yang.

After Mao died, 'The Gang of Four', including Mao's wife, who had masterminded the activities of the 'Red Guards' during the Cultural Revolution, soon fell. From then on, Mao's Communism was softened, to take account of the changing economic and political climate of China and the wider world. The CCP, however, maintained its grip on the state and its citizens.

Chapter 17

Philosophy after Mao

The Rise of a Market Economy

After the fall of the Gang of Four, the leadership of the
CPP was in the hands of Deng Xiaoping. His approach to
economic matters was distinctly pragmatic, and he
expressed his approval of elements of the capitalist
economy with the saying that the colour of a cat doesn't
matter, as long as it catches mice. Following this
approach, the CPP permitted market forces to come into
play in what had previously been a centralised Marxist
control economy, with increasing scope for private
entrepreneurs. By the mid 1980s the Chinese
government seemed to be managing a measured move
towards a consumer economy, and the material
conditions of many people began to improve. The
changes extended to the agricultural sector, with
peasant farmers regaining some rights to own their own
plots of land. But China was still politically Marxist-
Leninist, even if it was no longer Maoist.

The pro-democracy demonstration of 1989

Matters came to a head in 1989. Students in Beijing
initiated the well-known pro-democracy demonstration
in Tiananmen, the great square in front of the Forbidden
City, and for days they gathered around a large model of

the Statue of Liberty, demanding democratic reform of
the state. As is also well known, the demonstrations
were brutally suppressed by the authorities, and many
political figures, particularly in the education authorities,
were punished, right up to the then Party Secretary
Zhao Ziyang.

It is interesting to note not only that the Tiananmen
dispute was between two specifically non-Chinese
political-philosophical standpoints – democracy and
Marxism – but also that the response of the Chinese
authorities was also non-Chinese on at least three
counts. First, the troops who were ordered to suppress
the demonstrators refused their orders from the
government at least three times. Such refusals would
have involved heavy 'loss of face' on the part of Li
Peng, the Prime Minister who issued the order, and
this public failure would, in Chinese traditional terms,
have required his resignation. However, Li Peng
stayed in his post. Secondly, although the PLA had
attacked the enemy Nationalist and warlord forces,
on its way to victory in 1949, it was completely out of
character for it to use armed force against unarmed
civilians. Finally, the troops that actually cleared
Tiananmen were not those who had refused the earlier
action; they were reported to have been drafted in

from a border area that had a significant non-Han
Chinese population.

The Re-Emergence of Tradition

Whatever popular resentment there may have been
about the Tiananmen affair and the punishments that
followed, there was no significant revolt, and the system
continued with its mixture of Marxist-Leninist politics
and hybrid economic system. At the same time,
however, traditional Chinese thought was emerging
from its long hibernation of the Mao years. In the mid
1980s, editions of the Chinese classics were once again
on the bookstalls in Beijing. Confucian, Daoist and
Buddhist temples were not merely state-sponsored
museum sites, and some temples were training novices
in their schools. In April 1986 the Yingling Buddhist
Temple near Hangzhou was thronged with pilgrims
offering prayers and money and burning candles and
incense on the occasion of a Buddhist festival.

The 1990s also saw the rise of Christian sects, and
a movement known as Fa Lun Gong sprang up, based
on Chinese exercises and meditation with echoes of
Daoism and Buddhism. Clearly, among the devout and
the scholars, Chinese philosophical and religious ideas
were undergoing a renaissance, at the expense of the
state ideology of Marxism-Leninism.

Since the mid 1980s, the pace of economic relaxation
has increased. China developed Special Economic Zones
and by the beginning of 2008 was poised to become a
major world economic power. Chinese capital was
buying up mineral rights overseas, particularly in Africa,

and low-cost Chinese manufacturing was fuelling consumer spending across the developed world. Clearly, the colour of the cat just didn't matter.

Confucianism resurfaces

Despite the centralising effect on daily life during the heyday of CCP rule, the traditional family ties seem to have been preserved. Within a system that might be said to be attempting to impose a Mohist uniformity of care for everybody, the Confucian-inspired filial duties and obligations seem to have survived. Care for elderly parents is still widely practised, and indeed popular literature, such as the martial arts novels of Jin Yong, upholds Confucian values. Intellectuals such as Yu Dan who has published a self-help book on the *Analects* of Confucius and gives television talks about Confucian values, are turning to Confucianism as relevant to modern society. Universities are running courses on Confucianism, which are becoming more popular than those on Marxism, while secondary schools are including studies of the Chinese classics in their curricula. Professor Chen Lai of Beijing University has estimated that more than ten million Chinese children are studying the Confucian Classics. Some Chinese writers, for example Jiang Qing, argue that Confucianism is in fact a more appropriate system for China than Western liberal democracy, even going so far as to propose Confucianism as a state religion for China.

The resurgence of Confucianism can also be seen in Chinese official circles. In February 2005, the President, Hu Jintao, noted that 'Confucius said, 'Harmony is something to be cherished''', and later in the year he issued an instruction to Party cadres that they should seek to construct 'a harmonious society'. In 2006 the leading intellectual paper 'Southern Weekly' published an article discussing the term 'harmonious society' in terms of a quotation from Confucius, concluding that on this basis a welfare state needed to be founded on democracy and the rule of law. Then, in 2007 the Prime Minister, Wen Jiabao, said that the culture of China, from Confucius to Sun Yatsen, had 'numerous precious elements', including positive aspects relating to human nature and democracy. In Henan province, Communist Party officials are reported to be assessed on the basis of Confucian characteristics such as filial piety. Overseas, the Chinese government has sponsored a 'Confucian Institute' which has scores of campuses in dozens of countries.

Where Now?

This positive acknowledgement of a Confucian ethic, stressing social harmony at a time of rising internal disturbances, and perhaps reassuring the outside world of China's international goodwill, could be seen as a cynical ploy to pacify the population at a time when tens of thousands of individual civil disturbances are reported to have occurred. Time may well tell. At the time of writing, the world's economy is shrinking and recession is beginning to bite with no accurate prediction of how deep or how long it will be. China's economy in particular is being badly hit, judging by the steep diminution of its import of raw materials and fuel, and until consumer demand in the developed world recovers, the future for China's manufacturing industry is bleak. It is impossible to predict accurately what the social consequences of this will be for China as industrial unemployment rises.

The people of China have seen considerable change since the death of Mao, including the resurgence of Confucian ethics among the population and its acknowledgement by the CCP. In responding to the social and economic challenges of the global recession, the Chinese today are able to draw on the whole spectrum of ideas inherent in the neo-Confucian synthesis. The Confucian ideal of social responsibility, the Daoist concept of alignment with nature and reverence for the environment, the residual Legalist notion of order, and the spiritual insights into the human condition of Buddhism and Daoism offer a rich and universal resource with which to face troubled times.

Notes

1. (p. 44) That is, when society needed saving.
2. (p. 58) That is, 'not cruel'.
3. (p. 59) That is, a sense of 'right and wrong'.
4. (p. 61) This was the colour used by the Xia. Shang later used light-coloured sacrifices.
5. (p. 61) I have chosen the rendering 'augury' from the possible meanings for the character in the text since it appears to make sense of the preceding clause 'embellished like trees and grasses', which could easily describe a pattern of cracks in an oracle-bone divination.
6. (p. 63) That is, for marriage.
7. (p. 65) A *mu* is approx. a sixth of an acre, or a fifteenth of a hectare.
8. (p. 66) Whose salaries were paid in kind, including food.
9. (p. 66) Literally, 'the centre of the state' – here we are dealing with a city-state, which would have a central capital.
10. (p. 67) *Li*: a unit of distance, about one third of a mile.
11. (p. 94) Defined here as 'punishments, names, Regulations and Statecraft'.
12. (p. 94) A minister of the state of Qi in the Spring and Autumn period of the Zhou Dynasty
13. (p. 97) The character 德, 'virtue', is used here, and may indicate that the reward lay in being recognized as virtuous, and so liable to promotion.
14. (p. 103) Typically in grain or cloth.

Appendix

Timeline of Major Philosophers of Pre-Imperial China
(Dates to nearest decade)

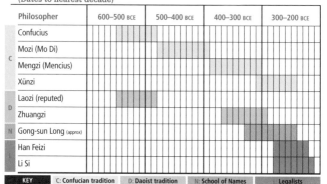

Philosopher	600–500 BCE	500–400 BCE	400–300 BCE	300–200 BCE
C	Confucius				
	Mozi (Mo Di)				
	Mengzi (Mencius)				
	Xūnzi				
D	Laozi (reputed)				
	Zhuangzi				
N	Gong-sun Long (approx)				
L	Han Feizi				
	Li Si				

KEY   C: Confucian tradition   D: Daoist tradition   N: School of Names   L: Legalists

Further Reading

Adelmann, F. J. *Contemporary Chinese Philosophy*. The Hague and Boston: M. Nijhoff, 1982.

Bell, Daniel A. *China's New Confucianism: Politics and Everyday Life in a Changing Society*. Princeton N.J.: Princeton University Press, 2008.

Confucius. *The Analects*. Trans. with intro., D. C. Lau. Harmondsworth: Penguin Books, 1979.

Fung Yu-lan. *A Short History of Chinese Philosophy*. Ed. Derk Bodde. First published 1948. Reprinted New York: Free Press, 1966.

Goldin, Paul R. *After Confucius: Studies In Early Chinese Philosophy*. Honolulu, HI: University of Hawai'i Press, 2005.

Graham, A. C. *Studies in Chinese Philosophy and Philosophical Literature.* (SUNY Series in Chinese Philosophy and Culture) Albany, NY: State University of New York Press, 1986.

Lai, Karyn L. *An Introduction to Chinese Philosophy*. Cambridge: Cambridge University Press, 2008.

Lao Tzu. *Tao te ching*. Trans. with intro., D. C. Lau. Harmondsworth: Penguin Books, 1963.

Mencius. Trans. D. C. Lau. Harmondsworth : Penguin, 1970.

Wilson, Andrew. *The 'Ever-Victorious Army': A History of the Chinese Campaign under Lt.-Col. C. G. Gordon, C.B. R.E. and of the Suppression of the Tai-ping Rebellion.* London: Greenhill Books, 1991.

Index

administration 36–7, 48, 49, 86
An Lushan 122–3
ancestor worship 13
animism 21
astrology 23

baihua script 156, 157
Beijing University 155, 158, 161
Book of Changes (*Zhou Li*) 37
Book of History (*Shu Jing*, *Book of Documents*) 37, 60, 62
Book of the Lord Shang 90
Book of Odes 37, 62, 63, 64, 72
Book of Rites 36
Boxer Rebellion 147–9
Britain 134–6
Bronze Age 15–16
Buddhism 9, 35, 114–25, 160
    arrival of 114–17
    emergence of a Chinese Buddhism 115–17
    origin of 132
    the rise of Buddhism from Han to Sui 117–18
    under the Tang 118–23
    worship of relics 124–5
bureaucracy 48, 104, 111
'burning of the books, the' 107–8

Chen Lai, Professor 161
Chen She 109
Cheng Hao 130
Cheng Yi 130
China
    isolation of 132
    unification of 78–9, 102–4
    Versailles Treaty 55
    war with Japan (1894–5) 145
    Western philosophy in 154

Chinese Communist Party (CCC) 156, 157, 158, 161, 162, 163
Chinese language/writing system 12–13, 81–5, 87, 105, 110–11, 150, 155–7
Chinese Republic 153
Chinese in the West 155–6
Christianity, Christians 133, 138, 147, 148
Communism 9, 156, 157
Confucianism 8–9, 15, 21, 36–49, 53–4, 59, 65, 69, 74, 79, 111, 121, 146
    consolidation of 124–5
    end of Confucian rule 153, 156
    in government 46–9
    Han 115
    mainstream 91
    'reformed' 78
    restored 113, 161–2
    Tang 126–9
Confucius 9, 15, 24, 29, 50, 51, 60, 64, 79, 80, 98, 111, 114, 146
    Analects (*Lun Yu*) 40–49, 57, 60, 62, 161
    life of 38–40
correct naming of things 77–8
Cultural Revolution 157

Da Yun Jing 121
Dao (Confucian) 42, 43, 48, 129
Dao Xue Jia 129
Dao-de Jing (*Laozi*) 24–9, 30, 33, 35, 96, 115
Daoism 8, 9, 15, 20, 24–9, 30, 31, 34, 35, 42, 44, 96, 114, 115, 120, 127, 128, 139, 160, 163
Deng Xiaoping 158
divination 13, 21–3, 32
Dynastic Histories 113

Eastern Zhou 36–7
Empress Dowager (Longyu) 152, 153
Empress Dowager Yehonala, 145, 146–9, 151–2
enlightenment 116, 117, 131
Ennin 132
Er Shi Huang Di 108
see also Ying Huhai

Fa Lun Gong 160
fa (Regulations) 94–7, 103, 104, 106, 112
Fa Xiang school 123
Feng Yünshan 139, 140
fengshui 23
filial piety 29, 42, 161–2
First World War 155
Five Classics 37
Five Element theory 23
Fu Xi 14

Gang of Four 157, 158
Gao Zong 120
Gao Zu 110, 118–19
see also Liu Bang
geography 11
Gong-sun Long 81–5, 86, 87
government regulation 104–6
Guang Xu, Emperor 145, 146, 148, 151
Guatama Buddha 116, 121, 125
Guo Moruo 156
Guo Xiang 30

Han Dynasty 110–13, 114, 115, 117
Han Fei 51–2, 79, 93–101, 102
Han state 88
Han Yu 124–5, 126–7, 129, 131
Hanfeizi 94–7
hexagrams 22
hierarchy versus universal love 54–5

Hong Xiuchuan 137–42
Hu Jintao 161–2
Hua Yan school 123
Huang Di (the Yellow Emperor) 14, 94
Hui Shi 80–81, 86
human nature as evil 73–4
human society, the nature of 75
'Hundred Days' of reforming legislation 146–7

India 35, 132

Japan 132
    Versailles Treaty 155
    war with China (1894–5) 145
Jesuits 133–4, 154
Jews 133

Kang Yuwei 146
Ketteler, Baron von 148
knights-errant (xie) 51–2, 54
Kong, Prince 144, 146

Laozi 24–5, 29, 30, 35, 94, 115
Legalism 79, 86, 102, 157, 163
    discredited 114
    evidence of the legalism of the Qin Empire 104–8
    Han Fei 93–8
    Li Si 98–9
    Shang Yang 90–93
    the state of Qin 99–101
    the Warring States 88–9
Legalists 74, 79, 87
Li Ao 128
Li Hongzhang 144, 146, 149, 150
Li Peng 159
Li Si 79, 93–4, 98–101, 102, 106, 108
    see also Qin Shi Huang Di
li (the Rites) 36, 37, 39, 43, 76–7, 89, 111, 117, 121, 130–31

Li Zhizao 154
Liang Qichao 149–50
Liezi 20, 32
Liu Bang 110
Liu Ying, Prince 114, 115
loyalty to one's superior 29

Macartney, Lord 135
Manchus 106, 134, 147, 152
    see also Qing Dynasty
Mandate of Heaven 60–64, 113, 118
Mao Zedong 156, 157, 163
market economy 158
Marxism 156, 161
Marxist-Leninism 157, 158, 160
Mencius (Mengzi) 56–69, 72, 79, 80, 127
    book of Mencius (Mengzi) 39, 56–60, 71
    goodness of human nature 58–9, 74, 130–31
    government 64–8
    Mandate of Heaven 60–64
    Mencius the man 56–7
    rebuttal of Mozi 68–9
milfoil stalks 22, 23
Ming, Emperor 114
Ming Dynasty 133, 142
model kings 14–15
Mohism 55
Mongols 129
Morrison, Robert 138
Mozi (Mo Di) 56, 68, 74, 80
    his arguments 53–5
    background 50–52
    Mencius' rebuttal of him 68–9
music 76–7
Muslims 133

neo-Confucianism 129–31, 131, 163
Neolithic culture 12–13, 15
Nestorian Christians 132
nirvana 116

occultism 13, 23, 25, 36, 123, 129
occultists 20
Opium War, First 136–7
Opium War, Second 136, 143, 144
oracle bones 13, 17–18, 22, 23, 32, 105

Pan Gu 14
physiognomy 23
Plato 130
portents 23
'Proclamation of Tang' 61–2
Pu Yi 151

Qian Long 135–6
Qin, Empire of
    collapse of the Qin Empire 109–10
    the death of Qin Shi Huang Di 108–9
    evidence of the legalism of the Qin Empire 104–8
    the rise of Han 110–13
    a unified China 102–4
Qin, state of 88, 92–4, 98, 99–101
Qin dynasty 79
Qin Shi Huang Di 102, 103, 104, 106, 108
    see also Li Si
Qing dynasty 134, 137, 149–53

'Rectification of Names' 46, 90
'Red Guard' 157
ren (humaneness) 29, 41, 42, 54, 58, 59, 64, 67, 131
'responsibility groups' 92–3, 103
Roberts, Reverend Issachar 140

sage, the 44–5
Sage Kings 45, 53, 56–7, 69, 78, 111, 112, 121, 146

Sanxingdui, Sichuan province 18
scapulimancy 17
scholars 51–2
School of Mind 130
School of Names 78, 80–87, 91
  Gong-sun Long and the White Horse debate 81–5
  the need to define things 80–81
  significance of 86–7
School of Principles 130
shamanism 13, 18, 21, 22, 32, 36, 123
Shang period 13, 16–19, 32, 36, 37, 61
Shang Yang 90–93, 99, 102, 127
Shen Nong 14
Shun (a Sage King) 14–15, 44, 45, 53
Si-ma Qian 18, 24, 30, 38, 39, 51, 52, 56, 57, 94, 98, 100, 112
Shiji 18, 70, 98, 100, 112–13, 157
Six Dynasties period 117–18, 124
Society of God 139, 140
Society of Heaven and Earth 137
Spring and Autumn Annals 37, 38
Statecraft 95, 112
Sui Dynasty 117
Sung Dynasty 125, 129, 130, 133
Sun Yat Sen 150, 153
Sunzi 57
sutras 115, 116, 121, 122, 123

Tai Ping rebellion 137–43, 144
Tai Ping Tian Guo ('Heavenly Kingdom of Great Peace') 141–2, 143
Tai Zong 119–20

Tang Confucianism 126–9
Tang Dynasty 118, 121, 123, 125, 129
Tang Liu Dian 121, 122
Tiananmen Square, Beijing demonstration (1989) 159–61
Tianzi ('the Son of Heaven') 47
tortoise shell divination 13, 17
tradition, re-emergence of 160–62
traditional institutions, the appeal of 106–8
trigrams 22

Unchanging Way 9

Versailles Treaty 55
virtue (de) 43–4
Voitinsky, Gregor 156

Waldersee, Count 148
Wang Guowei 154
Warring States period 37, 40, 48, 51, 56, 70, 88–9, 98, 106
Wei Changhui 140, 141
Wei state 88
weights and measures 105
'well field' system 65–7
Wen Jiabao 162
Western Zhou 19, 21, 23, 25, 36
White Horse debate 81–5
White Lotus sect 137, 147, 148
Wu, Empress 120–23
Wu Xian 32
wu-wei (non-action) 9, 26, 27

Xün (Xünzi; Xün Kuang) 71–9, 80, 86, 87, 91, 99, 110, 127
  the book of Xünzi 71–5, 93
  the importance of correct definitions 77–8

influence on philosophy 78–9
  the man 70–71
  a pragmatic approach to the Rites and music 76–7
Yang Zhu 20, 30, 68, 74
Yao (a Sage King) 14, 15, 44, 45, 53
Yehonala, Empress Dowager 145, 146–9, 151–2
Yen Fu 154
yi (righteousness) 29, 43, 54, 58, 59
Yijing (I Ching) 20–23
Yin Dynasty 32
Yin-yang theory 23
Ying Fusu 108
Ying Huhai 108
Yingling Buddhist temple 160
see also Er Shi Huang Di
Yu (a Sage King) 14, 15, 53, 69, 121
Yu Dan 161
Yu Qie 31, 32
Yuan, Lord 31–2

Zen (Chan) Buddhism 116
Zhao Gao (Middle Kingdom) 108–9, 135
Zhao state 88
Zhao Ziyang 159
Zheng, King 100, 101
zhi 59
Zhong Guo 134
Zhong Zhong 120, 121
Zhou Dynasty 19, 21, 37, 50, 88, 92, 121, 131
Zhouyi 22–3
Zhu Xi 130–31
Zhuang Xiang, King 100
Zhuang Zhou 34
Zhuangzi 30
Zhuangzi text 30–35, 80
Zoroastrians 132
Zuo Zhuan 38